Microsoft® Office Excel® 2010

Level 1

Microsoft® Office Excel® 2010: Level 1

Part Number: 084576
Course Edition: 1.01

NOTICES

DISCLAIMER: While Element K Corporation takes care to ensure the accuracy and quality of these materials, we cannot guarantee their accuracy, and all materials are provided without any warranty whatsoever, including, but not limited to, the implied warranties of merchantability or fitness for a particular purpose. The name used in the data files for this course is that of a fictitious company. Any resemblance to current or future companies is purely coincidental. We do not believe we have used anyone's name in creating this course, but if we have, please notify us and we will change the name in the next revision of the course. Element K is an independent provider of integrated training solutions for individuals, businesses, educational institutions, and government agencies. Use of screenshots, photographs of another entity's products, or another entity's product name or service in this book is for editorial purposes only. No such use should be construed to imply sponsorship or endorsement of the book by, nor any affiliation of such entity with Element K. This courseware may contain links to sites on the Internet that are owned and operated by third parties (the "External Sites"). Element K is not responsible for the availability of, or the content located on or through, any External Site. Please contact Element K if you have any concerns regarding such links or External Sites.

TRADEMARK NOTICES Element K and the Element K logo are trademarks of Element K Corporation and its affiliates.

Excel® 2010 is a registered trademark of Microsoft Corporation in the U.S. and other countries; the Microsoft products and services discussed or described may be trademarks of Microsoft Corporation. All other product names and services used throughout this course may be common law or registered trademarks of their respective proprietors.

Copyright © 2011 Element K Corporation. All rights reserved. Screenshots used for illustrative purposes are the property of the software proprietor. This publication, or any part thereof, may not be reproduced or transmitted in any form or by any means, electronic or mechanical, including photocopying, recording, storage in an information retrieval system, or otherwise, without express written permission of Element K, 500 Canal View Boulevard, Rochester, NY 14623, (585) 240-7500, (800) 478-7788. Element K Courseware's World Wide Web site is located at **www.elementkcourseware.com**.

This book conveys no rights in the software or other products about which it was written; all use or licensing of such software or other products is the responsibility of the user according to terms and conditions of the owner. Do not make illegal copies of books or software. If you believe that this book, related materials, or any other Element K materials are being reproduced or transmitted without permission, please call (800) 478-7788.

Element K is independent from Microsoft Corporation, and is not affiliated with Microsoft in any manner. While this publication and CD-ROM may be used in assisting individuals to prepare for a Microsoft Office Specialist (MOS) certification or MOS Expert certification exam, Microsoft, its designated program administrator, and Element K do not warrant that use of this publication and CD-ROM will ensure passing a MOS certification or MOS Expert certification exam.

What is the Microsoft Office Specialist Certification Program?

The Microsoft Office Specialist (MOS) Certification Program enables candidates to show that they have something exceptional to offer - proven expertise in Microsoft® Office programs. The MOS Certification Program is the only Microsoft-approved certification program of its kind. The MOS Certification exams focus on validating specific skill sets within each of the Microsoft® Office system programs. The candidate can choose which exam(s) they want to take according to which skills they want to validate. The available MOS exams include:

- MOS: Microsoft® Office Word 2010
- MOS: Microsoft® Office Excel 2010
- MOS: Microsoft® Office PowerPoint 2010
- MOS: Microsoft® Office Outlook 2010
- MOS: Microsoft® Office Access 2010
- MOS: Microsoft® SharePoint 2010

For more information:

To learn more about MOS or MOS Expert exams, visit **www.microsoft.com/learning/en/us/certification/mos.aspx**.

HELP US IMPROVE OUR COURSEWARE

Your comments are important to us. Please contact us at Element K Press LLC, 1-800-478-7788, 500 Canal View Boulevard, Rochester, NY 14623, Attention: Product Planning, or through our Web site at **http://support.elementkcourseware.com**.

Microsoft® Office Excel® 2010: Level 1

Lesson 6: Printing Excel Workbooks

Appendix A: Microsoft Office Excel 2010 Exam 77–882

About This Course

You possess some basic computer skills and are comfortable with using a computer to perform basic tasks. You may have used a calculator and paper to record data and perform calculations, and now want to migrate to using a computer application to store and process data in an electronic format. In this course, you will use Microsoft® Office Excel® 2010 to create spreadsheets that you can use to perform these tasks.

When manually calculating and recording data on paper, you need to recalculate every time you add new data. When working with large volumes of data, by the time the new set of data is recalculated manually, the paper-based sheets are a complete mess. Updating spreadsheets in Excel is easy and time saving. You can simply insert the new data and set the sheet to be updated whenever the data changes. Storing data electronically is more efficient because it allows you to quickly update existing data, run reports on the data, perform calculations, and much more.

Course Description

Target Student

This course is designed for students who desire to gain the necessary skills to create, edit, format, and print basic Microsoft Office Excel 2010 worksheets.

Course Prerequisites

To be successful in this course, you should be familiar with using personal computers and you should have used the mouse and keyboard. You should be comfortable in the Windows environment and be able to use Windows to manage information on the computer. Specifically, you should be able to launch and close programs; navigate to information stored on the computer; and manage files and folders. To ensure your success, we recommend you first take one of Element K's introductory Windows courses, such as either of the following, or have equivalent skills and knowledge:

- *Windows XP Professional: Level 1*
- *Windows XP: Introduction*

Course Objectives

In this course, you will create and edit basic Microsoft Office Excel 2010 worksheets and workbooks.

You will:

- Create a basic worksheet by using Microsoft Excel 2010.
- Perform calculations in an Excel worksheet.
- Modify an Excel worksheet.
- Modify the appearance of data within a worksheet.
- Manage Excel workbooks.
- Print the content of an Excel worksheet.

Certification

This course is designed to help you prepare for the following certification.

Certification Path: MOS: Microsoft Office Excel 2010 Exam 77–882

This course is one of a series of Element K courseware titles that addresses Microsoft Office Specialist (MOS) certification skill sets. The MOS and certification program is for individuals who use Microsoft's business desktop software and who seek recognition for their expertise with specific Microsoft products.

How to Use This Book

As a Learning Guide

This book is divided into lessons and topics, covering a subject or a set of related subjects. In most cases, lessons are arranged in order of increasing proficiency.

The results-oriented topics include relevant and supporting information you need to master the content. Each topic has various types of activities designed to enable you to practice the guidelines and procedures as well as to solidify your understanding of the informational material presented in the course.

At the back of the book, you will find a glossary of the definitions of the terms and concepts used throughout the course. You will also find an index to assist in locating information within the instructional components of the book.

In the Classroom

This book is intended to enhance and support the in-class experience. Procedures and guidelines are presented in a concise fashion along with activities and discussions. Information is provided for reference and reflection in such a way as to facilitate understanding and practice.

Each lesson may also include a Lesson Lab or various types of simulated activities. You will find the files for the simulated activities along with the other course files on the enclosed CD-ROM. If your course manual did not come with a CD-ROM, please go to **http://www.elementk.com/courseware-file-downloads** to download the files. If included, these interactive activities enable you to practice your skills in an immersive business environment, or to use hardware and software resources not available in the classroom. The course files that are available on the CD-ROM or by download may also contain sample files, support files, and additional reference materials for use both during and after the course.

As a Teaching Guide

Effective presentation of the information and skills contained in this book requires adequate preparation. As such, as an instructor, you should familiarize yourself with the content of the entire course, including its organization and approaches. You should review each of the student activities and exercises so you can facilitate them in the classroom.

Throughout the book, you may see Instructor Notes that provide suggestions, answers to problems, and supplemental information for you, the instructor. You may also see references to "Additional Instructor Notes" that contain expanded instructional information; these notes appear in a separate section at the back of the book. PowerPoint slides may be provided on the included course files, which are available on the enclosed CD-ROM or by download from **http://www.elementk.com/courseware-file-downloads**. The slides are also referred to in the text. If you plan to use the slides, it is recommended to display them during the corresponding content as indicated in the instructor notes in the margin.

The course files may also include assessments for the course, which can be administered diagnostically before the class, or as a review after the course is completed. These exam-type questions can be used to gauge the students' understanding and assimilation of course content.

As a Review Tool

Any method of instruction is only as effective as the time and effort you, the student, are willing to invest in it. In addition, some of the information that you learn in class may not be important to you immediately, but it may become important later. For this reason, we encourage you to spend some time reviewing the content of the course after your time in the classroom.

As a Reference

The organization and layout of this book make it an easy-to-use resource for future reference. Taking advantage of the glossary, index, and table of contents, you can use this book as a first source of definitions, background information, and summaries.

Course Icons

Icon	Description
	A **Caution Note** makes students aware of potential negative consequences of an action, setting, or decision that are not easily known.
	Display Slide provides a prompt to the instructor to display a specific slide. Display Slides are included in the Instructor Guide only.
	An **Instructor Note** is a comment to the instructor regarding delivery, classroom strategy, classroom tools, exceptions, and other special considerations. Instructor Notes are included in the Instructor Guide only.
	Notes Page indicates a page that has been left intentionally blank for students to write on.
	A **Student Note** provides additional information, guidance, or hints about a topic or task.
	A **Version Note** indicates information necessary for a specific version of software.

Course Requirements

Hardware

For this course, you will need one computer for each student and one for the instructor. Each computer will need the following minimum hardware components:

- 1 GHz Pentium-class processor or faster.
- Minimum 256 MB of RAM. 512 MB of RAM is recommended.
- 10 GB hard disk or larger. You should have at least 1 GB of free hard disk space available for the Office installation.
- CD-ROM drive.
- Keyboard and mouse or other pointing device.
- 1024 x 768 resolution monitor is recommended.
- Network cards and cabling for local network access.
- Internet access (contact your local network administrator).
- Printer (optional) or an installed printer driver.
- Projection system to display the instructor's computer screen.

Software

- Microsoft® Office Professional Plus 2010 Edition
- Microsoft® Office Suite Service Pack 1

● Microsoft® Windows® XP Professional with Service Pack 2

Class Setup

Initial Class Setup

For initial class setup:

1. Install Windows XP Professional on an empty partition.

    ■ Leave the Administrator password blank.

    ■ For all other installation parameters, use values that are appropriate for your environment (see your local network administrator for details).

2. On Windows XP Professional, disable the **Welcome** screen. (This step ensures that students will be able to log on as the Administrator user regardless of what other user accounts exist on the computer.)

    a. Click **Start** and choose **Control Panel→User Accounts.**

    b. Click **Change The Way Users Log On And Off.**

    c. Uncheck **Use Welcome Screen.**

    d. Click **Apply Options.**

3. On Windows XP Professional, install Service Pack 2. Use the Service Pack installation defaults.

4. On the computer, install a printer driver (a physical print device is optional). Click **Start** and choose **Printers and Faxes.** Under **Printer Tasks,** click **Add a Printer** and follow the prompts.

    If you do not have a physical printer installed, right-click the printer and choose **Pause Printing** to prevent any print error message.

5. Run the **Internet Connection Wizard** to set up the Internet connection as appropriate for your environment if you did not do so during installation.

6. Display known file type extensions.

    a. Right-click **Start** and then select **Explore** to open Windows Explorer.

    b. Choose **Tools→Folder Options.**

    c. On the **View** tab, in the **Advanced Settings** list box, uncheck **Hide Extensions For Known File Types.**

    d. Click **Apply** and then click **OK.**

    e. Close Windows Explorer.

7. Log on to the computer as the Administrator user if you have not already done so.

8. Perform a complete installation of Microsoft Office Professional 2010.

9. In the **User Name** dialog box, click **OK** to accept the default user name and initials.

10. In the **Microsoft Office 2010 Activation Wizard** dialog box, click **Next** to activate the Office 2010 application.

11. When the activation of Microsoft Office 2010 is complete, click **Close** to close the **Microsoft Office 2010 Activation Wizard** dialog box.

12. In the **User Name** dialog box, click **OK.**

13. In the **Welcome To Microsoft 2010** dialog box, click **Finish.** You must have an active Internet connection in order to complete this step. Here, you have to select the **Download And Install Updates From Microsoft Update When Available (Recommended)** option, so that whenever there is a new update, it gets automatically installed on your system.

14. After the Microsoft Update runs, in the **Microsoft Office** dialog box, click **OK.**

15. On the course CD-ROM, open the 084576 folder. Then, open the Data folder. Run the 084576dd.exe self-extracting file located in it. This will install a folder named 084576Data on your C drive. This folder contains all the data files that you will use to complete this course. If your course did not come with a CD, please go to **http:// elementkcourseware.com** to download the data files.

    Within each lesson folder, you may find a Solution folder. This folder contains solution files for the lesson's activities and lesson lab, which can be used by students to check their end results.

16. If necessary, minimize the **Language** bar.

Customize the Windows Desktop

Customize the Windows desktop to display the **My Computer** and **My Network Places** icons on the student and instructor systems.

1. On the desktop, right-click and choose **Properties.**

2. Select the **Desktop** tab.

3. Click **Customize Desktop.**

4. In the **Desktop Items** dialog box, check **My Computer** and **My Network Places.**

5. Click **OK** and click **Apply.**

6. Close the **Display Properties** dialog box.

Before Every Class

1. Log on to the computer as the Administrator user.

2. Delete any existing data file from the C:\084576Data folder.

3. Extract a fresh copy of the course data files from the CD-ROM provided with the course manual, or download the data files from **http://elementkcourseware.com.**

List of Additional Files

Printed with each activity is a list of files students open to complete that activity. Many activities also require additional files that students do not open, but are needed to support the file(s) students are working with. These supporting files are included with the student data files on the course CD-ROM or data disk. Do not delete these files.

1 | Getting Started with Excel

Lesson Time: 1 hour(s), 15 minutes

Lesson Objectives:

In this lesson, you will create a basic worksheet by using Microsoft Excel 2010.

You will:

- Identify the elements of the Excel interface.
- Navigate and select cells in worksheets.
- Customize the Excel interface.
- Create a basic worksheet.

Introduction

You often work with data, but may not be aware that Microsoft Excel 2010 enables users to store and manage data better. Knowing that using Excel 2010 has several advantages, you are ready to learn the details. In this lesson, you will familiarize yourself with the Excel 2010 environment, customize the interface, and create a basic worksheet.

Using an instrument without the basic knowledge of its components and operating procedures can be a complicated task. Similarly, it would be difficult to use a software application such as Excel without understanding its interface elements and tools. Excel 2010 provides an interactive interface with enhanced features that help you create professional workbooks to store and analyze data easily.

TOPIC A

Identify the Elements of the Excel Interface

You are interested in the efficiency that can be realized by using the Excel application for storing and manipulating data. Before you gain this efficiency, you need to be familiar with its interface. In this topic, you will identify the elements of the Excel interface.

Wouldn't it be easy to work at a new job if you were fully acquainted with the tasks involved? Similarly, exploring Excel's interface will help you familiarize yourself with the options available in the application, which in turn, will help you use the application effectively.

Microsoft Excel 2010

Excel is an application in the Microsoft Office suite that you can use to create, revise, and save data in a spreadsheet format. You can also add formulas and functions to perform calculations, and analyze, share, and manage information using charts and tables. Excel also has options for adding pictures, shapes, and screenshots to a spreadsheet.

The Excel Application window

When you launch Excel, two windows are displayed, one within the other. The outer window is the main *application window* that usually fills the entire screen, and provides various interactive tools and commands. The inner window is the *workbook window* where you will work with data.

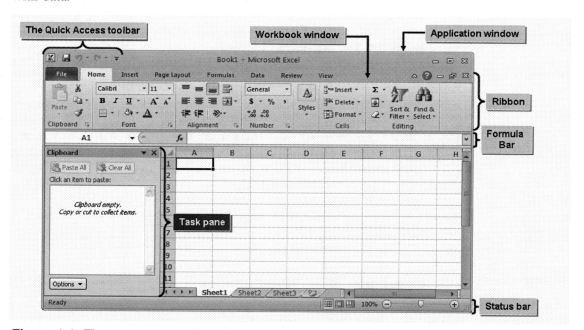

***Figure 1-1:** The components of an Excel application window.*

Component	Description
The Quick Access toolbar	A toolbar that provides you with an easy access to frequently used application commands.
The Ribbon	A panel that displays relevant commands to a particular set of tasks. These commands are organized into different tabs and groups.
The Formula Bar	A bar that displays the contents of the selected cell in a spreadsheet and can be used to type a formula or function. It also displays a reference to the active cell or the range of the current selection of cells.
The task pane	A pane that appears on an as-needed basis and provides you with several options for a particular command selected on the Ribbon. You can move and resize the task pane.
The status bar	A window element that is displayed at the bottom, and contains features such as dynamic zoom slider and a customizable status display.

The Ribbon

The *Ribbon* is an interface component that comprises several task-specific commands, which are grouped together under various tabs. It is designed to be the central location for accessing commands in the Microsoft Office suite for performing both simple and advanced operations without having to navigate extensively.

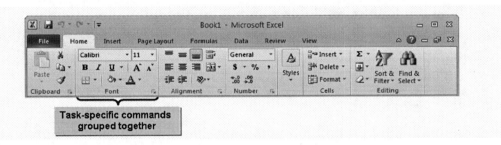

Figure 1-2: *The Ribbon displaying the commands of the Home tab.*

Ribbon Tab	Used To
File	Display the Backstage view that contains commands to print, save, and share workbooks.
Home	Format spreadsheet data, add basic data and cell formatting, and add styles.
Insert	Insert text, tables, charts, symbols, illustrations, and links.
Page Layout	Specify page settings, layout, orientation, margins, and other options related to printing a workbook.
Formulas	Create formulas with built-in functions to calculate values automatically. The built-in functions are categorized by the type of calculations they can perform.
Data	Connect with external data sources and import data for use within Excel worksheets.

Ribbon Tab	Used To
Review	Review Excel worksheets. It also provides tools such as spell checker, thesaurus, and translator.
View	Control the display of the worksheet and the workbook window. You can also hide or display the gridlines in a worksheet.

ScreenTips

A ScreenTip is descriptive text that is displayed when you position the mouse pointer over a component in the interface. An enhanced ScreenTip describes the component in detail and often provides a link to a help topic. Most of the components in Excel have associated enhanced ScreenTips. Excel provides you with options to select the level of detail you want ScreenTips to display. Additionally, there are options in the **Excel Options** dialog box to turn off the ScreenTips.

The Backstage View

The *Backstage view* is an interface element with options that group similar commands. This view is designed to simplify access to Excel features and can be used to save, send, print, open workbooks, display document information, and customize the application. You can access the Backstage view from the **File** tab.

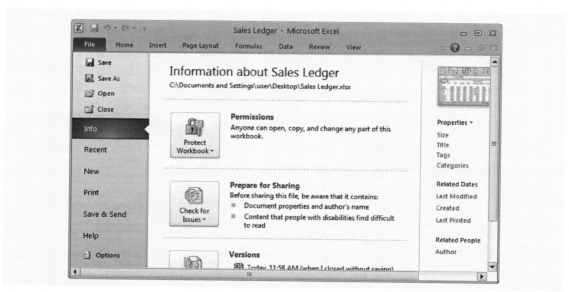

Figure 1-3: The Backstage view in Excel.

Option	Description
Save, Save As, Open, and **Close**	Allows you to save the changes made to a workbook, save a workbook with a new file name in the desired location, open an existing workbook, and close a workbook.
Info	Displays options to protect workbooks by using a password, check for accessibility and compatibility issues, manage versions of workbooks, and set workbook properties.

Option	Description
Recent	Lists workbooks that were recently accessed. It also allows you to customize the recently opened workbooks list by adding, removing, or reordering the items in the list.
New	Displays options to create a blank workbook, or a workbook based on a pre-defined or custom designed templates, or an existing workbook. You can also access additional templates from the Office.com website.
Print	Displays options to preview and print workbooks.
Save & Send	Provides options to save a workbook in a previous version of Excel, share a workbook through email or SharePoint, and publish a workbook.
Help	Allows you to access the online and offline help resources. It also provides access to the **Excel Options** dialog box.
Options	Displays the **Excel Options** dialog box, which allows you to customize the Excel interface.
Exit	Allows you to exit the application.

The Quick Access Toolbar

The *Quick Access toolbar* is usually located above the Ribbon and is displayed as an integrated component of the title bar. It provides easy access to commonly used commands such as **Save, Undo,** and **Redo.** The **Customize Quick Access Toolbar** menu options not only allow you to customize the display of buttons, but also reposition the Quick Access toolbar below the Ribbon. You can also add frequently used commands either from the Ribbon or by selecting options from the **Excel Options** dialog box.

Figure 1-4: The default commands on the Quick Access toolbar.

The Status Bar

The *status bar,* located at the bottom of the Excel application window, displays the current mode and cell information, such as average, count, and sum. It also has elements for adjusting the zoom level of the displayed worksheet and for selecting the desired page layout option.

Element	Function
The Mode indicator	Displays current mode of Excel along with the information of any special key, which is engaged.

Element	Function
The Auto Calculate indicator	Displays the average and sum of current selection along with the count of selected cells.
View buttons	Provides options to display a worksheet in any of the three default views: **Normal, Page Layout,** and **Page Break Preview.**
The **Zoom Out** button	Allows you to view the content in a worksheet in a smaller size.
The **Zoom** slider	Allows you to magnify or diminish a worksheet view to any desired size.
The **Zoom In** button	Allows you to enlarge the view of worksheet contents.
The **Zoom level** button	Allows you to set the zoom percentage of a worksheet.

The View Buttons on the Status Bar

The view buttons on the status bar enable you to view a worksheet in different views.

View Button	Allows You To
Normal	View a worksheet in the normal view.
Page Layout	View a worksheet as it will appear on a printed page.
Page Break Preview	View a preview of a worksheet where the pages will break when the worksheet is printed.

The Formula Bar

The *Formula Bar,* located below the Ribbon, contains the **Name Box,** the **Insert Function** button, and the **Formula Bar** text box. The **Name Box** displays the name or reference of the selected cells. The **Insert Function** button enables you to insert a function in the selected cell. The **Formula Bar** text box displays the contents of the selected cell and allows you to edit the contents. You can expand, collapse, resize, or hide the **Formula Bar** to suit your preferences.

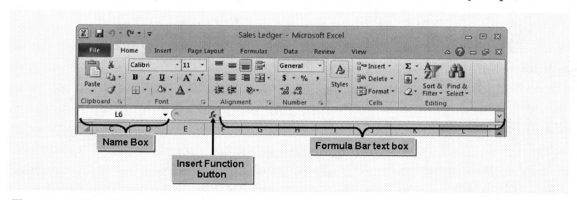

Figure 1-5: The Formula Bar on a worksheet.

Contextual Tabs

Contextual tabs are additional tabs that appear on the Ribbon when you select a specific object such as a chart, table, drawing, or text box. Because these tabs are context based, the commands displayed on the Ribbon depend upon the object that you select. These contextual tabs keep the number of tabs displayed on the Ribbon to a minimum and disappear once the relevant object is deselected.

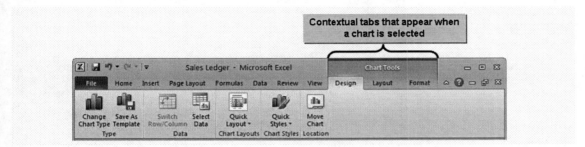

Figure 1-6: *A contextual tab displayed on the Ribbon.*

Templates

Definition:

A *template* is a predesigned layout that is used to create a document or a design pattern. A template can be created and stored in either an electronic or a print medium. Like most templates, an Excel template is a fixed layout, and you can make changes to the layout and customize it to create a new design pattern. Essentially, templates are created to simplify repetitive actions of creating similar looking documents.

Example:

Figure 1-7: *A template in Excel.*

The Excel Help Window

The *Excel Help window* enables you to search for information for your Excel-related questions and can be accessed by clicking the **Microsoft Excel Help** button at the top-right corner of the application window. You can also search Office.com for Excel-related information.

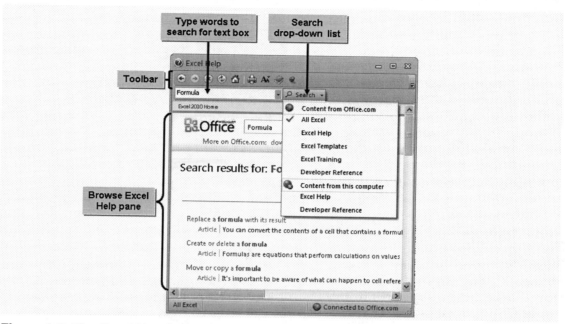

Figure 1-8: The Excel Help window.

Help Window Element	Description
The toolbar	Provides access to the navigation, printing, and formatting help contents.
The **Type words to search for** text box	Allows you to enter text to search for.
The **Search** drop-down list	Allows you to specify whether to search for the query term online or offline.
The **Browse Excel Help** pane	Displays links to various topics available in Excel Help. You can click a link to navigate to the desired topic.

Search Options

The **Search** drop-down list helps you narrow the search to a specific content repository. You can select an option from the list to restrict the search to your computer or include content from the Office.com website.

How to Identify the Elements of the User Interface

Procedure Reference: Open a Workbook Using the Open Dialog Box

To open a workbook using the **Open** dialog box:

1. Select the **File** tab and choose **Open** to display the **Open** dialog box.
2. Navigate to the desired file and click **Open.**

New Workbooks

You can select the **New** option on the **File** tab to open a new workbook. When you select **New,** the Backstage view displays the available templates organized in various categories from which to choose. You can choose to create a blank workbook, a workbook based on a template, or an existing workbook.

ACTIVITY 1-1
Identifying the Elements of the User Interface

Data Files:

C:\084576Data\Getting Started with Excel\Sales Revenue.xlsx

Scenario:

You have joined Our Global Company (OGC) Stores as a sales manager. In your job role, you need to use Excel application to analyze information. You have not worked with the Excel application previously; you want to familiarize yourself with the interface elements of the Excel application.

---

1. Explore the Backstage view and open a workbook.

    a. Choose **Start→All Programs→Microsoft Office→Microsoft Excel 2010** to launch the Microsoft Excel 2010 application.

    b. If necessary, in the **User Name** dialog box, click **OK**.

    c. In the **Welcome to Microsoft Office 2010** dialog box, select the **Don't make changes** option and click **OK**.

    d. On the Ribbon, select the **File** tab to display the Backstage view.

    e. Observe that the **File** menu consists of options to save, open, print, and close a workbook. From the menu, choose **New**.

    f. Under the **Available Templates** section, view the available templates and then from the **File** menu, choose **Open** to display the **Open** dialog box.

    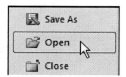

    g. Navigate to the C:\084576Data\Getting Started with Excel folder.

    h. Select the **Sales Revenue.xlsx** file and click **Open**.

---

2. Explore the Ribbon tabs.

a. On the Ribbon, select the **Page Layout** tab to view its commands.

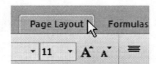

b. Observe that the **Themes, Page Setup, Scale to Fit, Sheet Options,** and **Arrange** groups are displayed along with the relevant commands.

c. In the **Page Setup** group, place the mouse pointer over any button to view its ScreenTip.

d. Select the other tabs on the Ribbon to view the commands and groups on them.

3. Explore the Quick Access toolbar.

a. On the Quick Access toolbar, place the mouse pointer over each button to view its description.

b. At the right end of the Quick Access toolbar, click the **Customize Quick Access Toolbar** drop-down arrow to display the **Customize Quick Access Toolbar** menu.

c. View the options available on the **Customize Quick Access Toolbar** menu and click the **Customize Quick Access Toolbar** drop-down arrow to close the menu.

4. Explore the status bar.

a.   On the status bar, to the left of the **Zoom** slider, place the mouse pointer over each of the buttons to view their descriptions.

b.   At the right end of the status bar, click the **Page Layout** button, which is the second button from the left, to change the layout of the worksheet.

c.   Click the **Page Break Preview** button which is located to the right of **Page Layout** button.

d.   In the **Welcome to Page Break Preview** message box, click **OK** to view the worksheet with page breaks.

e.   At the right end of the status bar, on the **Zoom** slider, click the **Zoom In** button.

f.   Observe that the zoom percentage has increased to 70%.

g.   Click the **Zoom Out** button and observe that the zoom percentage has reverted to 60%.

h.   Click the **Normal** button which is located to the left of **Page Layout** button to return to the normal view.

TOPIC B
Navigate and Select Cells in Worksheets

You familiarized yourself with the interface components of the Excel application. To view or modify data in Excel, you need to know how to work with worksheets. In this topic, you will navigate through an Excel worksheet.

Imagine that you have just moved to a new city to start a new job. To reach your office, you want to try the various modes of transport available in the city and decide on the quickest and the easiest option. Learning the basics of navigating in Excel is very similar to this; you know how to commute, but you need to familiarize yourself with the commuting options available. By navigating through Excel, you will familiarize yourself with the interface, thus making it easier for you to work with Excel.

Spreadsheets

Definition:

A *spreadsheet* is a paper or an electronic document that is used to store and manipulate data. It consists of rows and columns that intersect to form *cells,* where the data you enter is stored. Data can be in the form of numbers, text, and non-alphanumeric symbols in a tabular format. You can customize spreadsheets based on your business needs and data requirements.

Example:

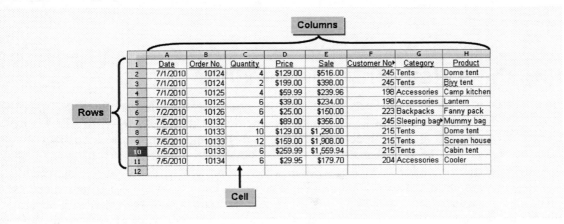

Figure 1-9: A spreadsheet with data.

Worksheets

A *worksheet* is an electronic spreadsheet that is used for entering and storing data in Excel. An Excel worksheet contains columns and rows, which intersect like a grid to form cells. Excel designates columns with alphabetical headers running across the top of the worksheet, and rows with numerical headers running down the left of the worksheet. An Excel worksheet can contain various types of data such as text, numbers, pictures, formulas, charts, or tables. You can insert or delete rows, columns, and cells from an Excel worksheet.

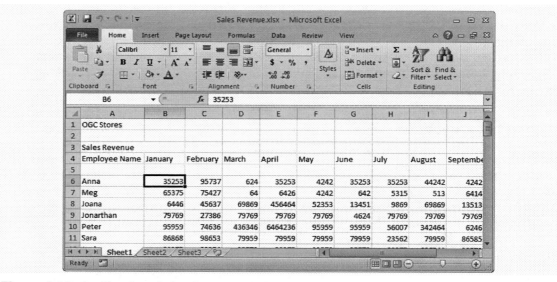

Figure 1-10: *An Excel worksheet.*

Worksheet Referencing Elements

Column headings in Excel worksheets begin with the letter A and continue through the letter Z. After the 26th column (column Z), headings become double letters, from AA to AZ. After AZ, the letter pairs start again with columns BA through BZ, and so on, until all 16,384 columns have alphabetical headings, ending with three-letter headers at XFD. Row headings begin with 1 and continue through 1,048,576. In Excel, cells are referenced based on the intersection of the respective column and row. For example, a cell in column B and row 3 is referenced as B3. The cell that is selected is called an *active cell* and the reference of the active cell appears in the **Name Box** on the Formula Bar. The contents of the active cell is displayed on the Formula Bar.

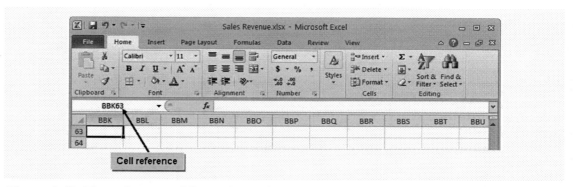

Figure 1-11: *The reference of the active cell in the Name Box.*

Workbooks

A *workbook* is an Excel file that acts as a repository for related Excel worksheets. The name of the workbook is displayed on the title bar of the Excel application window. By default, a new blank Excel workbook contains three worksheets: **Sheet1, Sheet2,** and **Sheet3.** The worksheet names are displayed on tabs at the bottom left of the workbook. You can rename, add, or delete worksheets in an Excel workbook.

Workbook Element	Description
The sheet tab bar	A bar at the bottom of a workbook that contains worksheet scroll buttons, worksheet tabs, and the **Insert Worksheet** button. It also contains the horizontal scroll bar.
The worksheet tabs	The tabs at the bottom left of the workbook that allow you to navigate across worksheets.
The tab scroll buttons	The buttons on the sheet tab bar, at the left of the worksheet tabs that provide you with options to scroll through the display of the worksheet tabs one at a time, or display the first or last grouping of the worksheet tabs in a workbook.
The **Insert Worksheet** button	The buttons on the sheet tab bar, at the right of the worksheet tabs that allow you to add a new worksheet to the workbook.

Mouse Navigation Options

You can use the mouse pointer to navigate through worksheets. You can also navigate to a specific cell within a worksheet, or to a different worksheet in a workbook.

Mouse Navigation Option	Action
Move the worksheet display up or down, one row	Click the top or bottom vertical scroll arrow.
Move the worksheet display left or right, one column	Click the left or right horizontal scroll arrow.
Move the worksheet display either horizontally or vertically	Click and hold the horizontal or vertical scroll arrow.

Move the worksheet display one screen at a time	Click the space between the scroll bar and the scroll arrow of either the vertical or the horizontal scroll bar.
Move rapidly through a worksheet	Drag either the vertical or the horizontal scroll bar.
Move to a specific cell in a worksheet	Click the **Name Box,** type the cell reference, and press **Enter.**
Display a different worksheet	Click the name of the desired worksheet on the sheet tab bar.

Keyboard Navigation Options

You can use a keyboard to navigate within and across worksheets in a workbook to enter, view, or modify data.

Keyboard Navigation Option	Action
Move one cell to the left, right, up, or down	Press the **Up, Down, Left,** or **Right** arrow key.
Move to column A of the current row	Press **Home.**
Scroll down or up by one screen	Press **Page Down** or **Page Up.**
Scroll one screen to the left or right	Press **Alt+Page Down** or **Alt+Page Up.**
Move to the cell on the right	Press **Tab.**

Move to the cell on the left	Press **Shift+Tab.**
Move to cell A1	Press **Ctrl+Home.**
Navigate across worksheets	Press **Ctrl+Page Up** or **Ctrl+Page Down.**
Move to the last column of the current row	Press **End.**
Move to the first or last column or row of data	Press **Ctrl** along with the **Up, Down, Left,** or **Right** arrow key.

Cell Selection Options

Excel provides you with multiple options to select a cell or a group of cells in a worksheet. You can select either a *contiguous range* consisting of cells that are adjacent to each other, or a *noncontiguous* range consisting of cells that are not adjacent to each other.

Selection Option	Action
A cell	Click the cell.
A contiguous range	Select the first cell in the range, hold down **Shift,** and select the last cell of the range. Alternatively, you can click and drag from the first cell of the range to the last cell of the range.
A noncontiguous range	Select the first cell in the first range, hold down **Ctrl,** and click the next cell in the range. To select multiple cells, hold down **Ctrl** and click multiple cells. You can also select multiple contiguous range of cells that are noncontinuous by using the Shift+click and Ctrl+click methods.
An entire row or column	Click the alphabetical header of a column or the numerical header of a row.
An entire worksheet	Click the Select All button below the **Name Box.**

How to Navigate and Select Cells in Worksheets

Procedure Reference: Navigate and Select Cells in a Worksheet

To navigate and select cells in a worksheet:

1. Open a workbook.

2. Use the appropriate navigation techniques to move to the desired location.

   ● Click in the **Name Box,** type the cell reference, and press **Enter** to move to a specific cell in the worksheet.

   ● Click the vertical or bottom scroll bar to move the worksheet display up or down.

   ● Press the **Up, Down, Left,** or **Right** arrow key to move one cell up, down, left, or right, respectively.

3. Use the appropriate selection methods to select cells.

   ● Click the cell to select the cell.

   ● Select the first cell in the range, hold down **Shift,** and select the last cell of the range.

   ● Click and drag from the first cell of the range to the last cell of the range to select a continuous range of cells.

ACTIVITY 1-2
Working with Cells in Excel

Before You Begin:
The Sales Revenue.xlsx file is open.

Scenario:
You want to familiarize yourself with the sales trend for your team to prepare a report on your team's performance for the past year. The sales information is stored in an Excel workbook. You need to view the relevant information of each sales person from this workbook.

---

1. View specific cells in the worksheet.

   a.   Scroll down to view the data in row 83.

   b.   Hold down **Ctrl** and press **Home** to navigate to the beginning of the worksheet.

   c.   Hold down **Ctrl** and press **Page Down** to move to the next worksheet.

   d.   Observe that **Sheet2** is selected.

   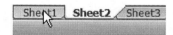

   e.   On the sheet tab bar, click **Sheet1** to return to the first worksheet.

---

2. Select a continuous range of cells.

   a.   Scroll down and select cell **A83**.

   b.   Hold down **Shift** and click cell **M84** to select a range of cells from A83 to M84.

   c.   At the top-left corner of the worksheet, below the **Name Box,** click the Select All button to select the entire worksheet.

   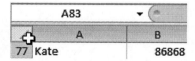

---

3. Select a noncontinuous range of cells.

   a.   Scroll up and select cell **A19.**

   b.   Hold down **Shift** and click cell **E19.**

   c.   Observe that the cells A19 to E19 are selected.

   d.   Hold down **Ctrl** and click cell **H19.**

   e.   Hold down **Shift** and click cell **J19.**

---

f.   Observe that a noncontinuous range of cells is selected.

g.   Click on any empty cell to deselect the selection.

TOPIC C

Customize the Excel Interface

You navigated through and selected content in an Excel worksheet. There may be instances when the default display and arrangement of the interface elements does not suit your preference. Excel provides you with options to personalize the interface according to your requirements. In this topic, you will customize the Excel interface.

When you start working with a new software application, the interface may not provide you with convenient access to all the options that you require, or the interface may be cluttered with options that you may not require at all. A cluttered interface can compromise your work efficiency. By customizing the application's interface, you will be able to access the options that you need easily and quickly.

The Excel Options Dialog Box

The **Excel Options** dialog box provides you with various options to customize the Excel user interface. These options are classified into 10 categories.

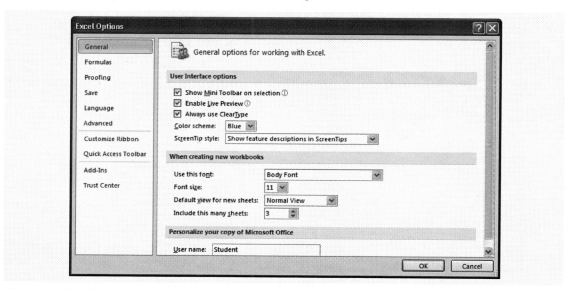

Figure 1-12: *The customizing options available in the Excel Options dialog box.*

Category	Description
General	Provides you with options to make general settings such as viewing the Mini toolbar, changing the color scheme of the Excel interface, and changing the ScreenTip style.
Formulas	Allows you to specify how to calculate formulas, manage performance, and control errors.
Proofing	Enables you to set the way Excel corrects and formats text.
Save	Provides you with options to customize the way workbooks are saved.
Language	Allows you to set the Office language preferences.

Category	Description
Advanced	Provides you with advanced options under various sections such as **Editing options, Image Size and Quality, Print,** and **Display.**
Customize Ribbon	Provides you with options to customize the Ribbon.
Quick Access Toolbar	Provides you with options to customize the Quick Access toolbar and include additional commands.
Add-Ins	Provides you with options to view and manage Office add-ins.
Trust Center	Provides you with access to information about protecting your privacy and securing your computer. It also allows you to specify the security and privacy settings.

How to Customize the Excel Interface

Procedure Reference: Customize the Quick Access Toolbar Using the Excel Options Dialog Box

To customize the Quick Access toolbar using the **Excel Options** dialog box:

1. Display the **Quick Access Toolbar** tab of the **Excel Options** dialog box.

   - Select the **File** tab and choose **Options,** and in the **Excel Options** dialog box, click **Quick Access Toolbar** or;

   - From the **Customize Quick Access Toolbar** menu, choose **More Commands.**

2. From the **Choose commands from** drop-down list, select the category from which you want to add a command.

3. In the **Choose commands from** list box, select the desired command and click **Add** to add the command to the Quick Access toolbar.

4. If necessary, click the **Move Up** or **Move Down** arrow button located on the right of **Customize Quick Access Toolbar** list box to move the options up or down the list.

 You can also reposition the Quick Access toolbar below the Ribbon by selecting the **Show Below the Ribbon** option from the **Customize Quick Access Toolbar** menu.

5. Click **OK** to close the **Excel Options** dialog box.

Procedure Reference: Customize the ScreenTip Style

To customize the ScreenTip style:

1. Select the **File** tab and choose **Options.**

2. If necessary, in the **Excel Options** dialog box, select the **General** tab.

3. Under the **User Interface options** section, from the **ScreenTip style** drop-down list, select an option.

   - Select **Show feature descriptions in ScreenTips** to display the name of the element along with a brief description.

   - Select **Don't show feature descriptions in ScreenTips** to display only the name of the element.

   - Select **Don't show ScreenTips** to disable ScreenTips.

4.   Click **OK** to apply the new ScreenTip style.

Procedure Reference: Add a Command Button from the Ribbon to the Quick Access Toolbar

To add a command button or group from the Ribbon to the Quick Access toolbar:

1.   On the Ribbon, select the tab that has the desired command button or group.

2.   Add the desired command button or group.

- Right-click the command button and choose **Add to Quick Access Toolbar.**

- Within the desired group, right-click the text region below the buttons and choose **Add to Quick Access Toolbar.**

Procedure Reference: Customize the Status Bar

To customize the status bar:

1.   At the bottom of the application window, right-click the status bar to display the **Customize Status Bar** menu.

2.   From the displayed menu, choose the required options.

 On the menu, when you choose an option, a check mark is displayed to its left to indicate that the selected option is displayed on the status bar. Selecting an option that has a check mark will hide the information on the status bar.

3.   Click away from the **Customize Status Bar** menu to close it.

Procedure Reference: Customize the Save Options

To customize the save options:

1.   Select the **File** tab and choose **Options.**

2.   In the **Excel Options** dialog box, select the **Save** tab.

3.   In the **Save workbooks** section, set the save options.

- From the **Save files in this format** drop-down list, select a format.

- In the **Save AutoRecover information every** text box, type the number of minutes to specify the duration after which AutoRecover information is saved.

- In the **Default file location** text box, type the path of the default location in which workbooks are saved.

4.   Click **OK** to apply the customized options.

Procedure Reference: Customize the Ribbon

To customize the Ribbon:

1.   Select the **File** tab and choose **Options.**

2.   In the **Excel Options** dialog box, select the **Customize Ribbon** tab.

3.   In the **Customize the Ribbon** list box, check or uncheck the check boxes for the tabs to show or hide the respective tab on the Ribbon.

4.   Create a new tab and group.

    a.   Below the **Customize the Ribbon** list box, click **New Tab** to create a tab.

    b.   If necessary, below the **Customize the Ribbon** list box, click **New Group** to create a group.

5. Rename a tab or a group.

    a. In the **Customize the Ribbon** list box, select the tab or group that you want to rename.

    b. Display the **Rename** dialog box.

        ● Below the **Customize the Ribbon** list box, click **Rename** or;

        ● Right-click the tab or group and choose **Rename.**

    c. In the **Rename** dialog box, type a new name and click **OK.**

6. Add commands to a group.

    a. From the **Choose commands from** drop-down list, select the desired category from which you want to choose commands.

    b. In the **Choose commands from** list box, select the desired command that you want to add.

    c. In the **Customize the Ribbon** list box, select the tab and group to which you want to add the command.

    d. Click **Add** to add the selected command.

7. If necessary, in the **Customize the Ribbon** list box, select a command and click **Remove** to remove the command from the group.

8. If necessary, create more tabs and groups and add commands to them.

9. Click **OK** to close the **Excel Options** dialog box.

ACTIVITY 1-3
Customizing the Microsoft Excel User Interface

Before You Begin:

The Sales Revenue.xlsx file is open.

Scenario:

You will be using the Excel application extensively in your role. You identified certain commands that you will use frequently and want a quicker option to access these commands. You also decide to display the required statistical information for the selected cells on the status bar. In addition, you need to maintain all official files in a specific folder.

1. Add the frequently used commands to the Quick Access toolbar.

   a. Click the **Customize Quick Access Toolbar** drop-down arrow, and from the displayed menu, choose **More Commands.**

   b. In the **Excel Options** dialog box, on the **Quick Access Toolbar** tab, in the right pane, in the **Choose commands from** list box, scroll down and select the **Open** option.

   c. Click **Add** to add the **Open** command to the Quick Access toolbar.

   d. In the **Choose commands from** list box, select the **New** option and click **Add** to add the **New** command to the Quick Access toolbar.

   e. From the **Choose commands from** drop-down list, select the **File Tab** option.

   f. In the **Choose commands from** list box, select **Close** and click **Add** to add the **Close** command to the Quick Access toolbar.

   g. Click **OK** to close the **Excel Options** dialog box.

h.   Observe that the newly added commands are displayed on the Quick Access toolbar.

2.   Add the **Alignment** group to the Quick Access toolbar.

a.   On the Ribbon, select the **Home** tab.

b.   In the **Alignment** group, right-click on the text "Alignment" and choose **Add to Quick Access Toolbar.**

c.   On the Quick Access toolbar, click the **Alignment** button to display the options in the **Alignment** group.

d.   Observe that all the **Alignment** group options are now accessible from the Quick Access toolbar and then click the **Alignment** button to close the **Alignment** group.

3.   Customize the status bar.

a.   On the status bar, right-click to view the **Customize Status Bar** menu.

b.   From the displayed menu, choose **Macro Recording.**

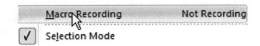

c.   Observe that a check mark is displayed beside the **Macro Recording** option denoting that **Macro Recording** is added to the status bar and the macro recording icon is displayed in the status area of the status bar.

d.   Choose **Maximum** and **Minimum** to add them to the status bar.

e.   From the displayed menu, choose **Zoom.**

f.   Observe that the check mark is removed and the zoom percentage that was displayed on the status bar is hidden.

g.   Click away from the menu to close the **Customize Status Bar** menu.

4.   Set the default location and color scheme.

a.   Select the **File** tab and choose **Options.**

b. In the **Excel Options** dialog box, verify that the **General** tab is selected.

c. In the **User Interface Options** section, from the **Color scheme** drop-down list, select **Blue.**

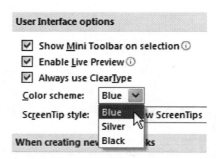

d. In the **Excel Options** dialog box, select the **Save** tab.

e. In the **Save workbooks** section, in the **Default file location** text box, triple-click and type *C:\084576Data* and click **OK.**

f. Observe that the blue theme is applied.

g. On the Quick Access toolbar, choose **Close** to close the file.

TOPIC D
Create a Basic Worksheet

You customized the Excel interface to enable easy access to frequently used commands in Excel. To start using the Excel application, you need to add data to a worksheet and save it. In this topic, you will enter data in an Excel worksheet.

Bricks are put together to construct a building, and complex structures are achieved by combining the bricks in different forms. Similarly, basic data are put together to create complex worksheets. Before you begin to create complex worksheets, you should know how to enter basic data.

Data Types

Excel allows you to enter various types of data. These data types can be generally categorized as labels, values, and dates and time. Labels are text that can be represented using letters, numbers, and symbols. Values are numbers that you may use to perform mathematical or statistical analysis. Date and time are used to represent date, time, or both in various formats. Depending on the data you enter in a cell, Excel automatically chooses the appropriate data type.

Excel 2010 File Formats

The default file type in Excel 2010 is (.xlsx) an XML-based file format. Files saved in this format are suffixed with the letter x. Using this XML-based file format allows files to be automatically compressed upon saving and decompressed upon opening. Saving spreadsheets in the default Excel 2010 file format not only allows you to secure data, but also recover data if the file is corrupt. Excel provides you with an extensive list of formats to save spreadsheets that can be shared with other users.

File Type	Description
Excel Workbook (.xlsx)	The default file type in Excel 2010.
Excel Macro-Enabled Workbook (.xlsm)	A basic XML file type that can store VBA macrocode.
Excel 97–2003 Workbook (.xls)	The file type that is used to save a file in a format that is compatible with the previous versions of Excel.
Excel Template (.xltx)	The default file type for an Excel template. It is used to save a workbook as a template so that new workbooks can be created using its content, layout, and format.

Excel Macro-Enabled Template (.xltm)	The default file type for an Excel macro-enabled template.
Excel Binary Workbook (.xlsb)	The binary file format in Excel 2010.

| Excel 97–2003 Template (.xlt) | The file type that enables you to save an Excel template that is compatible with the previous versions of Excel. |
| PDF (.pdf) | The file type that enables you to save an Excel document as an Adobe Portable Document Format (PDF) file. |

The Save and Save As Commands

The **Save** command is used to save a new workbook or the changes made to an existing workbook, without altering its name, file type, or location. The **Save As** command is used to save an existing file with a new name, file type, or location. These commands can be accessed from the **File** tab.

 If you use the **Save** command when a workbook was not previously saved, the **Save As** dialog box will be displayed automatically.

The Save As Dialog Box

The **Save As** dialog box can be used to select a different folder, in which to save the file. The default name of the file is displayed in the **File name** text box. You can also specify a different file name for the file. From the **Save as type** drop-down list, you can select a different format in which to save the file.

The Compatibility Checker Feature

The *Compatibility Checker feature* in Excel 2010 allows you to identify the compatibility of objects and data in an Excel 2010 workbook, when you intend to save it in an earlier version of Excel. In the **Microsoft Excel - Compatibility Checker** dialog box, you can view a list of features in your Excel 2010 file that are not supported in earlier versions of Excel. The dialog box also provides you with an option to convert these objects so that they are visible in earlier versions of Excel. However, you will not be able to modify the objects once you convert them.

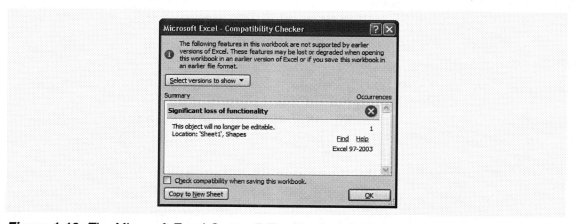

Figure 1-13: The Microsoft Excel Compatibility Checker dialog box.

How to Create a Basic Worksheet

Procedure Reference: Create a Workbook and Enter Data

To create a workbook and enter data:

1. Select the **File** tab and choose **New.**

2. In the Backstage view, in the **Available Templates** pane, below the **Home** button, select **Blank workbook.**

3. In the right pane, in the **Blank workbook** pane, click **Create.**

4. In the new worksheet, enter the desired data.

5. Use the appropriate navigation technique to select the next cell where you want to enter data.

6. From the **File** tab menu, choose **Save.**

Procedure Reference: Perform a Compatibility Check on a Workbook

To perform a compatibility check on a workbook:

1. Select the **File** tab and choose **Info.**

2. In the Backstage view, in the **Prepare for Sharing** section, from the **Check for Issues** drop-down list, select **Check Compatibility.**

3. In the **Microsoft Excel – Compatibility Checker** dialog box, observe the features that are not supported in the earlier version of Excel and click **Cancel.**

Procedure Reference: Save a Workbook Using the Save As Option

To save a workbook using the **Save As** option:

1. Select the **File** tab and choose **Save As** to display the **Save As** dialog box.

2. In the **Save As** dialog box, navigate to the desired folder.

3. In the **File name** text box, type a name for the file.

4. From the **Save as type** drop-down list, select the desired file format and click **Save.**

 If you select a format of an earlier version of Excel, the Compatibility Checker feature will automatically check the file for any compatibility issues.

5. If necessary, in the **Microsoft Excel - Compatibility Checker** dialog box, click **Continue** to convert the features that are not supported in the earlier version of Excel.

Procedure Reference: Recover Unsaved Workbooks

To recover unsaved workbooks:

1. On the **File** tab, select **Recent.**

2. In the Backstage view, in the right pane, select the **Recover Unsaved Workbooks** option.

3. In the **Open** dialog box, select the unsaved workbook and click **Open.**

ACTIVITY 1-4

Entering Data in an Excel Workbook

Scenario:

OGC Stores has recently introduced two new products. You have the sales data for these products on a printed paper. You want to create an invoice with this data in an Excel worksheet to send it to a customer. You also need to send a copy of this invoice to a coworker in the accounting department who is using Excel 2003.

---

1. Enter the column headings.

    a. On the Quick Access toolbar, click **New** to open a blank workbook.

    b. In cell A1, type **Product** and press **Tab** to move to cell B1.

    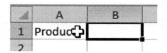

    c. In cell B1, type **Quantity** and press **Tab.**

    d. In cell C1, type **Price** and press **Tab.**

    e. In cell D1, type **Date of Shipment** and press **Enter.**

---

2. Enter the name of the products.

    a. Click cell **A3,** type **Pen** and press **Enter.**

    b. In cell A4, type **Chart**

---

3. Enter the data for quantity.

    a. Click cell **B3,** type **410** and press **Enter.**

    b. In cell B4, type **385**

---

4. Enter the price and date of shipment.

    a. Click cell **C3,** type **0.5** and press **Enter.**

    b. In cell C4, type **2**

    c. Enter today's date in cells D3 and D4.

---

5. Save the workbook in different file formats.

a.   Select the **File** tab and choose **Save.**

b.   Navigate to the C:\084576Data\Getting Started with Excel folder.

c.   In the **Save As** dialog box, in the **File name** text box, triple-click and type *My Invoice* and click **Save.**

d.   Select the **File** tab and choose **Save As.**

e.   In the **Save As** dialog box, from the **Save as type** drop-down list, select **Excel 97–2003 Workbook (*.xls)** and click **Save** to save the file in the XLS format.

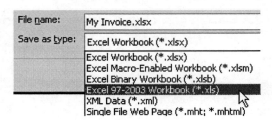

f.   On the Quick Access toolbar, click **Close** to close the file.

Lesson 1 Follow-up

In this lesson, you identified the elements of the Excel environment and created a basic worksheet. This knowledge will enable you to work with the various options available in the Excel interface.

1. **What advantages do you see for using Excel to store data?**

2. **In your estimation, which options in the Backstage view will allow you to perform tasks with ease?**

2 | Performing Calculations in an Excel Worksheet

Lesson Time: 45 minutes

Lesson Objectives:

In this lesson, you will perform calculations in an Excel worksheet.

You will:

- Create formulas in a worksheet.
- Insert functions in a worksheet.
- Reuse formulas.

Introduction

You created a basic worksheet and entered data in it. Now, you are ready to work with data that contains trends and patterns to be analyzed. To identify these trends and patterns, you need to perform some calculations based on the data. In this lesson, you will perform calculations in an Excel worksheet.

Performing calculations manually can be tedious and prone to errors. However, you can use Excel's formulas and built-in functions to perform data calculations quickly and free of errors.

TOPIC A
Create Formulas in a Worksheet

You entered data in an Excel worksheet. You may need to perform calculations based on formulas to analyze the data further. In this topic, you will create formulas in Excel.

Calculating the values of data in worksheets manually can be time consuming and may even lead to inaccurate or erroneous results. Excel provides you with an easier and quicker way to calculate accurate values by creating formulas that help you automate calculations.

Formulas

Definition:

A *formula* is a symbolic representation that defines the standard procedure for a calculation. A formula comprises an expression to the right and a resultant to the left of an equal sign. The expression in a formula usually consists of a combination of variables, constants, and operators.

Example:

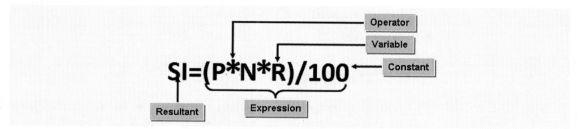

Figure 2-1: A mathematical formula to compute Simple Interest.

Excel Formulas

An Excel formula is a type of formula that can be used to perform calculations on data that is entered in Excel worksheets. All formulas in Excel begin with an equal sign and contain various components such as arguments and operators. The result of an Excel formula is stored in the cell where the formula is entered. When the data of the arguments in an Excel formula changes, the formula automatically recalculates the result. You can revise existing formulas by pressing **F2** and changing the arguments in the formula.

An Excel formula has various elements.

Formula Element	Description
References	Addresses of cells or ranges of cells on a worksheet that refer to the location of the values or data on which you need to apply a formula for calculation.
Operators	Symbols that specify the kind of calculation that needs to be performed on the components of a formula.
Constants	Numbers or text that do not change in a formula.
Functions	Predefined formulas in Excel that are used to simplify complex calculations.

Mathematical Operators

Mathematical operators are symbols or signs that are used to represent an arithmetic operation in Excel.

Mathematical Operator	Function
Plus sign (+)	Add
Minus sign (-)	Subtract
Asterisk (*)	Multiply
Forward slash (/)	Divide
Caret symbol (^)	Exponent
Open and closed parentheses	Group computation instructions

Order of Evaluation

Excel allows you to create formulas that contain multiple mathematical operators. These mathematical operators are computed in a specific order. When you use a combination of operators, the order of evaluation can affect the result of the formula. Excel evaluates the mathematical operators in the following order.

1. Computations enclosed in parentheses, wherever they appear in the formula.

2. Computations involving exponents.

3. Computations involving multiplication and division. Because they are equal with regard to the order in which Excel performs them, the operation is performed in the order in which it encounters them, which is from the left to the right.

4. Computations involving addition and subtraction. Excel also performs them in the order in which it encounters them.

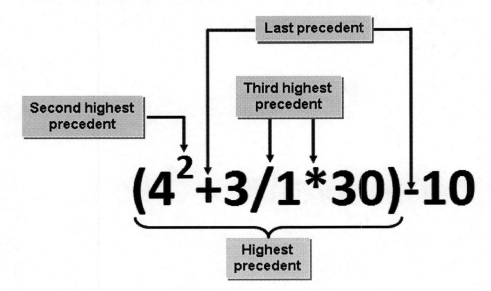

Figure 2-2: Operators computed in a specific order.

Enforcing Precedence with Parentheses

You can use parentheses to group expressions within another expression. When an expression is within parentheses, it means that it is evaluated first and the result is used to evaluate the remainder of the expression. If there are nested sets of parentheses, then the innermost set is evaluated first.

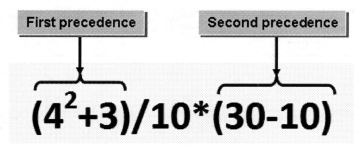

Figure 2-3: *A formula displaying precedence within parentheses.*

How to Create Formulas in a Worksheet

Procedure Reference: Create a Formula

To create a formula:

1. Select the cell in which you want to enter a formula.
2. Type the formula.
    a. Type the equal sign.
    b. Specify the arguments and operators for the formula.
        ● Enter a number or cell reference, or select a cell.
        ● Enter the operator.
        ● If necessary, enter another argument.
    c. If necessary, enter additional arguments and operators to complete the formula.
3. Press **Enter** to apply the formula and populate the cell with the calculated value.

ACTIVITY 2-1
Creating Formulas

Data Files:

C:\084576Data\Performing Calculations in an Excel Worksheet\New Product Sales.xlsx

Scenario:

The management of OGC Stores has planned to introduce four new products in the market. You need to determine the profitability of these products by analyzing the estimated sales data, expenses, and tax.

---

1. Calculate the total income for the products.

   a.   Navigate to the C:\084576Data\Performing Calculations in an Excel Worksheet folder and open the New Product Sales.xlsx file.

   b.   Select cell **B8**.

	A	B
1		
2		
3	**Income**	
4	Specialty coffee baskets	2560
5	Cheese baskets	1342
6	Fruit baskets	3795
7	Assortment baskets	6790
8	Total Income	
9	Expenses	5035

   c.   Type **=B4+B5+B6+B7** and press **Enter** to display the total income of the products.

   =B4+B5+B6+B7

   d.   Observe that the sum of the values in the cell range B4:B7 is displayed in cell B8.

2560
1342
3795
6790
14487

---

2. Calculate the net income for the products.

   a.   Select cell **B10**.

b. Type = and select cell **B8**.

◢	A	B
1		
2		
3	**Income**	
4	Specialty coffee baskets	2560
5	Cheese baskets	1342
6	Fruit baskets	3795
7	Assortment baskets	6790
8	Total Income	14487
9	Expenses	5035
10	Net Income	=B8

c. Type - and select cell **B9**.

◢	A	B
1		
2		
3	**Income**	
4	Specialty coffee baskets	2560
5	Cheese baskets	1342
6	Fruit baskets	3795
7	Assortment baskets	6790
8	Total Income	14487
9	Expenses	5035
10	Net Income	=B8-B9

d. Observe the formula displayed on the Formula Bar and press **Enter**.

3. Calculate the tax and profit after tax for the products introduced in the market.

    a. Verify that cell B11 is selected.

    b. Type *=B10*E2* and press **Enter**.

	=B10*E2

    c. Observe that the tax calculated by multiplying the net income with the tax rate is displayed in cell B11.

◢	A	B	C	D	E
1					
2				Tax Rate:	3%
3	**Income**				
4	Specialty coffee baskets	2560			
5	Cheese baskets	1342			
6	Fruit baskets	3795			
7	Assortment baskets	6790			
8	Total Income	14487			
9	Expenses	5035			
10	Net Income	9452			
11	Tax	283.56			

d. Calculate the profit after tax in cell B12 by deducting the net income in cell B10 from the tax in cell B11.

10	Net Income	9452
11	Tax	283.56
12	Profit After Tax	9168.44

 Observe that a green triangle appears at the top-left corner of the cell when Excel finds the formula in the cell to be inconsistent with the other formulas in the column. Select the cell with the green triangle and click the **Error Checking** button that appears, and from the menu, choose **Ignore Error.**

e. Select the **File** tab and choose **Save As.**

f. In the **Save As** dialog box, in the **File name** text box, type *My New Product Sales* and click **Save.**

g. Close the workbook.

TOPIC B

Insert Functions in a Worksheet

You created formulas to perform simple calculations on the data in a worksheet. To perform complex calculations to analyze data, you need to use more complex formulas. In this topic, you will use Excel's built-in functions to perform complex calculations.

You can create formulas to perform complex calculations on the data in a worksheet. However, using functions for routine calculations is even more user friendly because you do not have to type the entire formula each time. Excel provides you with various built-in functions that you can use to analyze data.

Functions

Definition:

A *function* is a built-in Excel formula that can be used to perform calculations. Functions contain a *function name,* followed by *arguments* within parentheses. The function name is usually an abbreviated name of the function. Function arguments can be cell references, constants, formulas, other functions, or logical values.

Example:

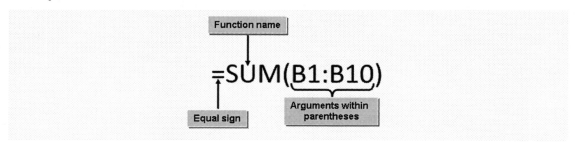

Figure 2-4: A function comprising arguments.

Function Categories

Functions in Excel are categorized by their purposes. There are 12 categories of functions.

Category	Used To
Financial	Perform common business calculations, such as determining the repayment for a loan, the future value or net present value of an investment, or a schedule of cash flow.
Date & Time	Work with date and time values in functions.
Math & Trig	Perform mathematical calculations.
Statistical	Perform statistical analysis on data. It includes the average, highest and lowest values, median, standard deviation, and other statistics functions.
Look up & Reference	Find values in a list or table, or used when you need to find a reference to a cell.

Category	Used To
Database	Query lists of data held in a worksheet. The calculations will be done on records that meet the specified criteria.
Text	Manipulate textual values.
Logical	Check whether a condition is true or false.
Information	Return the formatting, location, or contents of a cell.
Engineering	Perform engineering analysis.
Cube	Analyze the contents of a database to learn more about your business. It represents sets of data derived from raw information stored in a standard database.
Compatibility	Develop spreadsheet applications that are compatible with earlier versions of Excel.

The Formula AutoComplete Feature

The Formula AutoComplete feature is a dynamic feature in Excel that allows you to conveniently choose and enter functions without having to remember lengthy function names or risking a spelling error. When you type the equal sign, followed by the first few characters of a function, a drop-down list with all the available function names beginning with the same characters will be displayed. You can select the required function from the list and enter the necessary arguments.

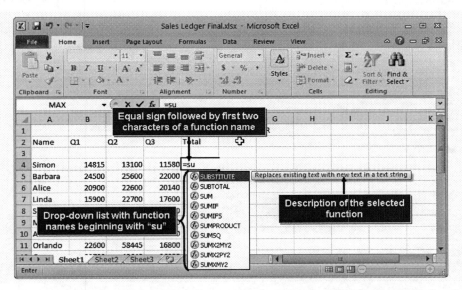

Figure 2-5: The Formula AutoComplete feature listing functions beginning with "su."

Commonly Used Functions

Excel provides you with various built-in functions that you can frequently use to work with data.

Function	Enables You To
SUM	Add all the values specified in the argument.
AVERAGE	Calculate the average of the values specified in the argument.
MIN	Find the lowest of the values specified in the argument.
MAX	Find the highest of the values specified in the argument.
COUNT	Find the number of cells that contain numerical values in the specified range in the argument.
COUNTA	Find the number of cells that contain data within a specified range. This function does not count the empty cells.

The AutoSum Feature

The *AutoSum feature* allows you to quickly insert commonly used functions in a worksheet to perform basic mathematical and statistical analysis. You can also use this feature to build formulas that compute the average value, count the number of values, and return the highest or lowest values specified in a range.

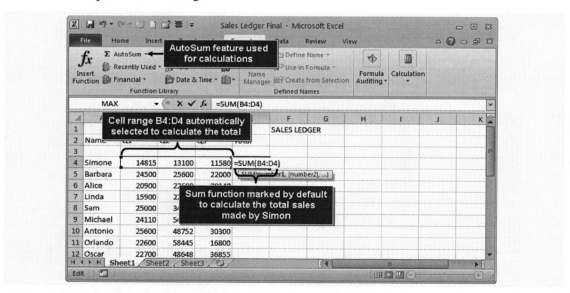

Figure 2-6: *The AutoSum feature used to calculate a total.*

How to Insert Functions in a Worksheet

Procedure Reference: Apply a Formula by Using the Formula AutoComplete Feature

To apply a formula by using the Formula AutoComplete feature:

1. Select the cell in which you want to enter a formula.
2. In the worksheet, type the equal sign and the first few letters of the function name.
3. In the AutoComplete list, double-click a function to select it and enter the formula.
4. Specify the arguments for the function.
5. Press **Enter** to apply the formula.

Procedure Reference: Insert Functions

To insert functions:

1. Select the cell in which you want to enter a formula.
2. On the Ribbon, select the **Formulas** tab.
3. Display the **Insert Function** dialog box.
   - In the **Function Library** group, click **Insert Function** or;
   - On the Formula Bar, click the **Insert Function** button.
4. Select a desired function.
   - In the **Search for a function** text box, type a brief introduction of what you want to do and click **Go.**
   - From the **Or select a category** drop-down list, select a category.
5. In the **Select a function** list box, select the desired function and click **OK.**
6. In the **Function Arguments** dialog box, enter the desired arguments.
7. At the bottom left of the **Function Arguments** dialog box, preview the displayed formula result and click **OK.**

Procedure Reference: Calculate Values by Using the AutoSum Feature

To calculate values by using the AutoSum feature:

1. Enter the values that you want to calculate in the cells.
2. Click on the cell where you want the result to appear.
3. Display the result.
   - Apply the sum function.
     - On the **Home** tab, in the **Editing** group, click the **AutoSum** button or;
     - On the **Formulas** tab, in the **Function Library** group, click the **AutoSum** button.
   - Apply other functions.
     - On the **Home** tab, in the **Editing** group, click the **AutoSum** drop-down arrow, and from the displayed list, select a function or;
     - On the **Formulas** tab, in the **Function Library** group, click the **AutoSum** drop-down arrow, and from the displayed list, select a function.

4. Ensure that the selected range of cells is correct.

- If it is correct, press **Enter.**
- If it is incorrect, drag the selection to the range of cells you want to include in the calculation and press **Enter.**

ACTIVITY 2-2
Calculating Values Using Functions

Data Files:

C:\084576Data\Performing Calculations in an Excel Worksheet\Sales Ledger.xlsx

Scenario:

You want to analyze the sales performance of the employees for the three quarters and calculate the total sales for each sales person. You also want to determine the sales data of the best performer and the average sales per sales person for the three quarters.

---

1. Calculate the total sales made by Simon and Barbara for Q1 through Q3.

    a. Navigate to the C:\084576Data\Performing Calculations in an Excel Worksheet folder and open the Sales Ledger.xlsx file.

    b. Select cell **E4**.

◢	A	B	C	D	E
1					
2	Name	Q1	Q2	Q3	Total
3					
4	Simon	14815	13100	11580	

    c. On the **Home** tab, in the **Editing** group, click the **AutoSum** button. $\boxed{\Sigma \cdot}$

    d. Observe that the cell range B4:D4 is selected.

4	Simon	14815	13100	11580	=SUM(B4:D4)
5	Barbara	24500	25600	22000	SUM(number1, [number2], ...)

    e. Press **Enter** to display the total sales made by Simon for Q1 through Q3.

4	Simon	14815	13100	11580	39495

    f. Similarly, calculate the total sales made by Barbara for Q1 through Q3.

5	Barbara	24500	25600	22000	72100

---

2. Calculate the average sales made by Simon and Barbara.

a. Select cell **F4** and type **=av**

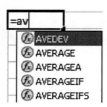

b. In the AutoComplete list, double-click **AVERAGE.**

c. In the worksheet, select the cell range **B4:D4** and press **Enter** to display the sales average.

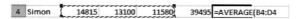

d. Similarly, calculate the average sales made by Barbara for Q1 through Q3.

---

3. Calculate the highest sales made by Simon and Barbara.

a. Select cell **G4.**

b. Select the **Formulas** tab, and in the **Function Library** group, click **Insert Function.**

c. In the **Insert Function** dialog box, in the **Search for a function** text box, type **Max** and click **Go.**

d. In the **Select a function** list box, verify that **MAX** is selected and click **OK.**

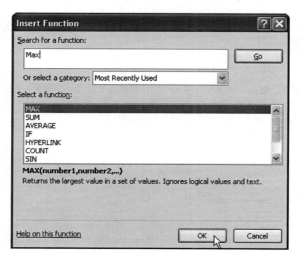

e. In the **Function Arguments** dialog box, to the right of the **Number1** text box, click the **Collapse Dialog** button, and select the cell range **B4:D4.**

f.   Click the **Expand Dialog** button, 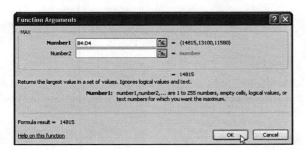 and then click **OK**.

g.   Similarly, calculate the highest sales for Barbara for Q1 through Q3.

4.   Calculate the lowest sales made by Simon and Barbara.

a.   Select cell **H4.**

b.   On the **Formulas** tab, in the **Function Library** group, click the **AutoSum** drop-down arrow, and from the displayed list, select **Min.**

c.   In the worksheet, select the cell range **B4:D4** and press **Enter** to display the lowest sales made by Simon.

d.   Similarly, calculate the lowest sales for Barbara for Q1 through Q3.

5.   Save the worksheet.

a.   Select the **File** tab and choose **Save As.**

b.   In the **Save As** dialog box, in the **File name** text box, type *My Sales Ledger* and click **Save.**

c.   Close the workbook.

TOPIC C
Reuse Formulas

You calculated data by using Excel formulas and functions. Sometimes, you may need to use the same calculation to analyze data in a different cell of a worksheet. In this topic, you will copy formulas and functions to reuse them.

When working with data in an Excel worksheet, you may want to reuse the formulas and functions to apply in similar cells across the worksheet. Typing the formulas and functions every time you need to use them is very tedious. Excel allows you to copy formulas and functions to the required cells.

The Cut, Copy, and Paste Commands

Excel allows you to move or copy cells and their contents in a worksheet. You can select a cell or its content and move it using the cut and paste options. To copy the content of a cell, you can use the copy and paste options. Excel provides you with the paste preview feature that enables you to view how the content will appear on the spreadsheet before you actually paste it.

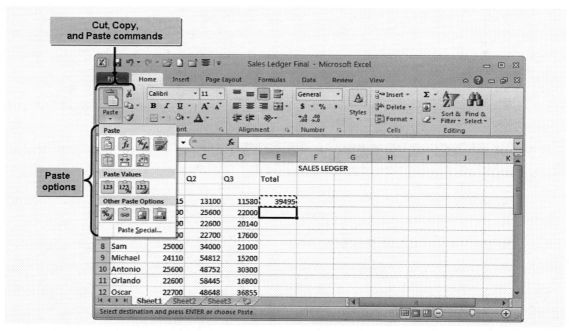

Figure 2-7: *The Cut, Copy, and Paste commands used to reuse data.*

Paste Special Options

You can copy and paste specific cell contents or attributes such as formats, formulas, and values by using the **Paste Special** option in Excel. By selecting the appropriate **Paste Special** option, you can reuse a specific property of the selected cell.

Paste Special Option	*Enables You To*
Paste	Paste the content with the formula and formatting.
Formulas	Paste all the text, numbers, and formulas in the current selection without the format of the source cell.
Formulas and Number Formatting	Paste the content with the number formats and formulas.
Keep Source Formatting	Paste the content with the formatting that was applied to the source cell.
No Border	Paste the content in the cell without any borders if the source cell had any borders.
Keep Source Column Width	Paste the content and keep the column width the same as the source cell.
Transpose	Paste the content by transposing rows into columns or columns into rows.
Values	Paste the calculated value of the formula used in the source cell.
Values and Number Formatting	Paste the calculated value of the formula used in the source cell along with the number formatting.
Values and Source Formatting	Paste the calculated value of the formula used in the source cell along with the formatting.
Formatting	Paste only the formatting applied to the source cell.
Operations	Paste the results of the mathematical calculations based on the value of the source cell. <ul><li>The **Add** option will add the value of the source cell to the destination cell.</li><li>The **Subtract** option will subtract the value of the source cell from the destination cell.</li><li>The **Divide** option will divide the value of the source cell with the destination cell.</li><li>The **Multiply** option will multiply the value of the source cell with the destination cell.</li></ul>
Comments	Paste only the comments that are attached to the source cell.
Validation	Paste only the data validation rules applied to the source cell.
Paste as a Link	Paste a reference to the source cell so that the value of the destination cell is linked to the value of the source cell.

Live Preview

Live Preview is a dynamic feature of Excel that allows you to preview how a formatting will appear on a worksheet before you actually apply it. For example, when you move the mouse pointer over various options in the **Font** drop-down list, you can see a live preview of how each font option will affect the appearance of the selected cell without actually applying the font to the object. However, this temporary formatting is removed when the mouse pointer is moved away from the selected option.

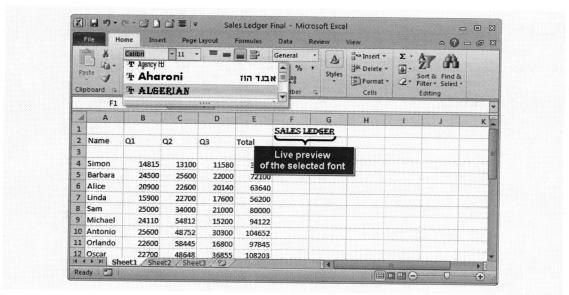

Figure 2-8: Preview of how a formatting will appear on a worksheet.

Relative References

Definition:

A *relative reference* is a cell reference in a formula that changes when a formula is copied from one cell to another, based on the new position of the formula. Relative references are used to create formulas that use values, which are stored in a cell that is relative to the cell in which the result is to be displayed.

Example:

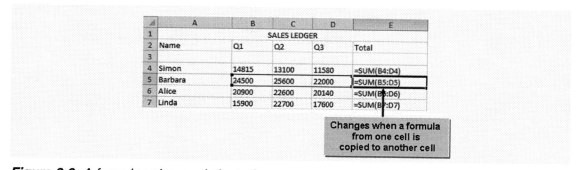

Figure 2-9: A formula using a relative reference.

Absolute References

Definition:

An *absolute reference* is a cell reference in a formula that does not change when the formula is copied from one cell to another. Absolute references are used in formulas to refer to the values in cells whose reference does not change in relation to the cells where the result is to be stored. Absolute references contain a dollar sign before the column and row headings in the cell reference.

Example:

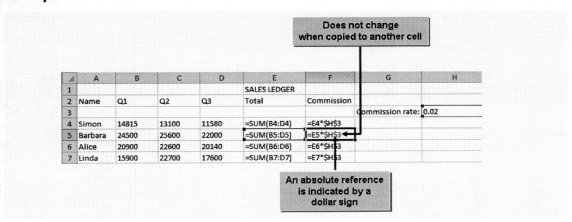

Figure 2-10: A formula using an absolute reference.

Mixed References

A *mixed reference* is a cell reference that contains a mix of absolute and relative references. When a formula with a mixed reference is copied from one cell to another, the relative reference changes, while the absolute reference does not change. Mixed references contain a dollar sign either before the column or the row reference.

How to Reuse Formulas

Procedure Reference: Copy a Formula or Function

To copy a formula or function:

1. Select the cell that contains the formula you want to copy.
2. On the **Home** tab, in the **Clipboard** group, click **Copy.**
3. Select the destination cell where you want to paste the formula.
4. In the **Clipboard** group, click **Paste.**

The Cut, Copy, and Paste Shortcut Keys

The following table identifies the shortcut keys for the **Cut, Copy,** and **Paste** options.

Action	Shortcut Key
Cut	Ctrl+X
Copy	Ctrl+C
Paste	Ctrl+V

Procedure Reference: Create an Absolute Reference

To create an absolute reference:

1.   Select the cell with the formula that needs to refer to constant cell values.

2.   On the Formula Bar, in the **formula box,** click and type the dollar sign in front of the column and row references to make the cell reference constant in the formula.

 You can press **F4** on the keyboard to add the $ sign in front of the column and row references.

3.   Press **Enter** to apply the change made to the formula.

ACTIVITY 2-3
Copying Formulas and Functions

Data Files:

C:\084576Data\Performing Calculations in an Excel Worksheet\Sales Ledger Final.xlsx

Scenario:

Your manager has asked you for information on the commission earned by your team. You want to calculate the commission earned by your sales team for the three quarters. For each employee, the formula for calculating the commission should reference the commission rate value that is specified in the worksheet.

---

1. Calculate the commission for the employees based on the commission rate.

    a. Navigate to the C:\084576Data\Performing Calculations in an Excel Worksheet folder and open the Sales Ledger Final.xlsx file.

    b. Select cell **I4**, type *=E4*L3* and press **Enter**.

    > `=E4*L3`

    c. Select cell **I4**, select the **Home** tab, and in the **Clipboard** group, click **Copy**.

    d. Select cell **I5**, and on the **Home** tab, in the **Clipboard** group, click **Paste**.

    e. Observe that cell I5 displays the value 0 because the formula used in cell I4 now references to cell L4.

---

2. Modify the formula to use an absolute reference to the cell containing the commission rate.

    a. Select cell **I4**, and in the **Formula Bar** text box, click immediately before "L" and press **F4**.

    > `=E4*$L$3`

    b. Observe that the $ sign is added before the column and row references and press **Enter**.

    c. Select cell **I4**, and on the **Home** tab, in the **Clipboard** group, click **Copy**.

    d. Select cell **I5**, and in the **Clipboard** group, click **Paste**.

    e. Observe that the cell value in cell I5 has changed and the cell reference for the commission rate remains the same.

    f. Save the file as *My Sales Ledger Final*

    g. Close the workbook.

Lesson 2 Follow-up

In this lesson, you performed calculations in an Excel worksheet. By using the formulas and built-in functions in Excel, you can perform calculations easily and quickly, and without any errors.

1.   **Which built-in functions in Excel do you expect to use the most often?**

2.   **Do you think the Formula AutoComplete feature is beneficial to you? Why?**

3 | Modifying a Worksheet

Lesson Time: 45 minutes

Lesson Objectives:

In this lesson, you will modify an Excel worksheet.

You will:

● Edit worksheet data.

● Find and replace data.

● Manipulate worksheet elements.

Introduction

You entered formulas and functions in Excel worksheets to perform calculations. When you work with worksheets, you will often need to update data in them. In this lesson, you will modify the content of an Excel worksheet.

To modify a paper-based spreadsheet, you may have to re-create the entire spreadsheet to include new additions or other changes. Excel minimizes the effort required to revise and update spreadsheets. By using Excel, you can easily modify the data in an existing worksheet, rather than creating a new worksheet every time you need to change data.

TOPIC A
Edit Worksheet Data

You performed calculations in an Excel workbook, which enables you to interpret data better. There may be instances when you have to work with existing worksheets, and you need to alter the data presented in them. In this topic, you will edit the data in an Excel worksheet.

Suppose you join a company, and you are asked to create an expense report for the year by using Excel. You will not set out to create a report from scratch, rather you may use an existing report as a base and edit its various data to create a new report. You can use various Excel options to edit data, which will enable you to complete the tasks quickly and efficiently.

The Undo and Redo Commands

The **Undo** command allows you to reverse the most recent actions that you performed on a workbook. The **Redo** command allows you to cancel the most recent **Undo** actions. You can access these commands from the Quick Access toolbar or by using the shortcut keys, **Ctrl+Z** for **Undo** and **Ctrl+Y** for **Redo.** The **Undo** drop-down list displays all the recently performed actions that can be reversed, and the **Redo** drop-down list displays all the recently undone actions. You can undo or redo several actions at once by selecting the actions from these lists. However, some actions such as saving a workbook cannot be undone.

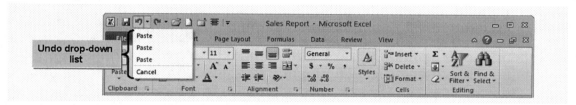

Figure 3-1: The Undo drop-down list listing actions that can be undone.

The Auto Fill Feature

The *Auto Fill feature* allows you to fill cells with a series of data. You can enter data in one or more cells to establish a pattern for the series, select the cells, and drag the *fill handle* to fill the cells with the series. The fill handle is the box at the bottom-right corner of the selected cell or cell range. You can specify how the data should be filled in the target cells by using the options on the **Auto Fill Options** menu.

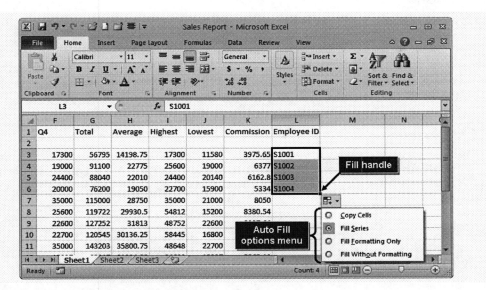

Figure 3-2: *Data entered using the Auto Fill feature.*

Auto Fill Options

The Auto Fill options in Excel 2010, help you specify how a selected range of cells should be filled in with data.

Auto Fill Option	*Allows You To*
Copy Cells	Fill the selected range with the selected data in a cell or cells.
Fill Series	Fill the selected range with the series of data specified by the pattern in the selected cells.
Fill Formatting Only	Fill the selected range with only the formatting used in the selected cell, but not the data.
Fill Without Formatting	Fill the selected range with the data in the selected cell, but without the formatting that is applied to that data.

Other Auto Fill Options

The Auto Fill options vary according to the data in the first cell of the selected range of cells. For instance, when a day is typed in the first cell, the **Auto Fill Options** menu will display the **Fill Days** and **Fill Weekdays** options. You can then select an option to include or exclude the weekends from the series, as required.

The Copy Cells Option

The **Copy Cells** option on the **Auto Fill Options** menu allows you to copy data to the destination cell or range of cells. The **Copy Cells** option simplifies the procedure to copy content by allowing the paste action to be repeated for the selected range.

The Transpose Option

The **Transpose** option in the Paste command shifts the vertical and horizontal orientation of the columns and rows in a worksheet. For example, if data is set up with months as rows and department names as columns, the **Transpose** option will reverse the rows and columns when the data is pasted so that the months become columns and the department names become rows.

Clear Options

The **Clear** button on the **Home** tab in the **Editing** group provides you with options to clear formatting, data, or comments from the cells in a worksheet. You can also choose **Clear All** to remove all the data at once.

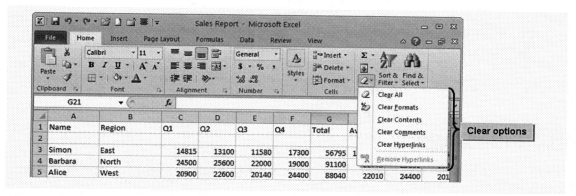

Figure 3-3: *The Clear drop-down list displaying clear options.*

Clear Option	Used to Clear
Clear All	Everything from the selected cells including contents, formatting, data, and comments.
Clear Formats	Only the formatting applied to the selected cells.
Clear Contents	Only the contents in the selected cells.
Clear Comments	Comments attached to the selected cells.
Clear Hyperlinks	Hyperlinks from the selected cells.

How to Edit Worksheet Data

Procedure Reference: Edit Cell Data

To edit cell data:

1. Select the cell that contains the data you want to edit.
2. Edit the cell data.
   - Type the new data in the cell and press **Enter** to replace the cell data or;
   - Click the contents displayed on the Formula Bar and edit the data to update the cell data.
3. Type the new data in the cell and press **Enter.**

Procedure Reference: Fill Cells with a Series of Data Using the Auto Fill Feature

To fill cells with a series of data by using the Auto Fill feature:

1. Enter the required data to establish a pattern for the series of data.
2. Select the cells with the values that has established the pattern.
3. Drag the fill handle to the ending cell of the series.
4. If necessary, click the **Auto Fill Options** drop-down arrow and select an option to fill cells.

Procedure Reference: Clear Cell Data

To clear cell data:

1. Click in a cell and type the data.
2. Edit the data in the cell.
   a. Double-click the cell and type the new data or;
   b. Select the cell that contains the data to be edited and then type the new data.
3. Clear the cell data.
   - Select the cell that contains the data to be edited and press **Delete.**
   - Select a range of cells whose data has to be cleared, and on the **Home** tab, in the **Editing** group, click the **Clear** button and select the appropriate clear option.

Procedure Reference: Move Data Between Cells

To move data between cells:

1. Select the cells that contain the data you want to move.
2. Move the selected cells.
   - Position the mouse pointer on the selection border until the mouse pointer changes to a copy/move pointer and drag the selection to the destination or;
   - On the **Home** tab, in the **Clipboard** group, click the **Cut** button, select the cell to which you want to move the data, and click **Paste.**

Procedure Reference: Transpose Data

To transpose data:

1. Select the data that you want to transpose.

2. Copy the data to the clipboard.

- Cut the selected cells to transpose the data.

- Copy the selected cells to transpose a copy of the data.

3. Select the destination cell in which you want the transposed data to appear.

4. On the **Home** tab, in the **Clipboard** group, from the **Paste** drop-down list, select the **Transpose** option.

Procedure Reference: Use the Undo and Redo Commands

To use the **Undo** and **Redo** commands:

1. Perform an action in a worksheet.

2. Undo the action.

- On the Quick Access toolbar, click the **Undo** button to undo one action.

- On the Quick Access toolbar, click the **Undo** drop-down arrow, and from the displayed list, select the desired actions to undo several actions.

3. If necessary, redo undone the action.

- On the Quick Access toolbar, click the **Redo** button to redo one action.

- On the Quick Access toolbar, click the **Redo** drop-down arrow, and from the displayed list or undone actions, select the desired actions to redo several actions.

ACTIVITY 3-1
Manipulating Data

Data Files:

C:\084576Data\Modifying an Excel Worksheet\Sales Report.xlsx

Scenario:

You presented the worksheet that includes a summary of the sales data of your team to the management. The management has suggested the following changes, which you want to implement in the worksheet.

1. Add the IDs of all the employees.

2. Change the region of an employee who has been recently transferred.

3. Delete the ID of an employee who has left the company.

4. Display the names of the employees in a single row in a new worksheet.

---

1. Enter the IDs of all the employees.

   a. Navigate to the C:\084576Data\Modifying an Excel Worksheet folder and open the Sales Report.xlsx file.

   b. Scroll to the right, click cell **L3**, type **S1001** and press **Enter** to enter the ID of the first employee.

K	L
ommission	Employee ID
3975.65	S1001
6377	
6162.8	

   c. Select cell **L3** and click and drag the fill handle to cell L20 to fill in the corresponding cells with the employee IDs of the other employees.

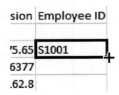

    d.   Observe that the IDs of the other employees are filled in the respective cells by automatically increasing the numeric value of the first employee's ID by 1.

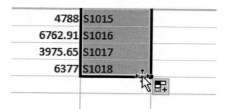

2.   Edit the employee details.

    a.   Scroll to the left and select cell **B8,** type *West* and press **Enter.**

    b.   Scroll to the right and select cell **L9.**

    c.   On the **Home** tab, in the **Editing** group, at the bottom left corner, click the **Clear** drop-down arrow and select **Clear All.**

3.   Move the contents of the cells.

    a.   Scroll left and select the cell range **A22:B22.**

    b.   On the **Home** tab, in the **Clipboard** group, click **Cut.**

    c.   Scroll to the right and select cell **O4,** and in the **Clipboard** group, click **Paste.**

4.   Transpose the contents from a column to a row in a different worksheet.

    a.   Scroll to the left and select the **A3:A20** cell range.

    b.   On the **Home** tab, in the **Clipboard** group, click the **Copy** button.

    c.   Click **Sheet2.**

d. Verify that cell A1 is selected, and in the **Clipboard** group, from the **Paste** drop-down list, in the **Paste** section, click the **Transpose** button which is the last.

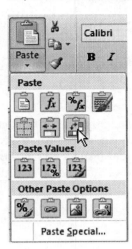

e. Observe that the names of the employees, which were displayed in rows in Sheet1 are copied and transposed to columns in Sheet2.

f. Save the worksheet as ***My Sales Report***

TOPIC B
Find and Replace Data

You edited the data in a worksheet. When you have a worksheet with a large volume of data, it would be difficult for you to identify and update only specific values. In this topic, you will search and replace specific data in a worksheet.

When you need to update specific data in a worksheet, you can manually search for that data by visually examining each cell in the worksheet. This is a time-consuming and tiresome process, and you may also end up not locating the data altogether. Excel provides you with options to quickly and accurately locate and change the required data and ensure that the worksheet is free of any spelling mistakes.

Cell Names

You can name a cell or a range of cells to identify it by the name you specify, rather than using the cell reference. Cell names are not case sensitive and can be up to 255 characters long, but they cannot contain spaces or begin with a number. When you want to move to a named cell or range of cells, enter the name of the cell in the **Name Box** and press **Enter** or display the **Name Box** drop-down list and select the name.

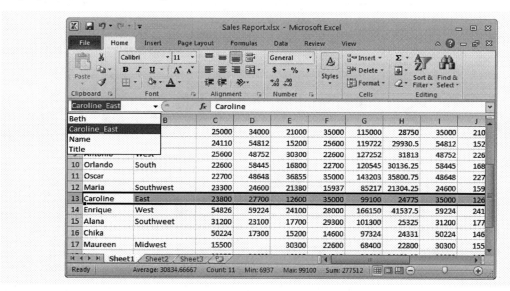

Figure 3-4: A named cell range.

The Find Command

The **Find** command allows you to locate specific data within a workbook. The **Find** tab of the **Find and Replace** dialog box contains various options that allow you to perform the search.

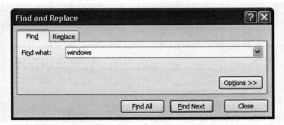

Figure 3-5: *The Find tab of the Find and Replace dialog box.*

Option	Description
The **Find what** drop-down arrow	Displays all the recently searched terms.
The **Options** button	Provides advanced search options such as specifying the search location or matching the text casing.
The **Find All** button	Allows you to locate all the instances of the search term's occurrence.
The **Find Next** button	Allows you to search for the next occurrence of the search term.
The **Close** button	Allows you to close the **Find and Replace** dialog box.

Access the Find Command

You can access the **Find** command from the **Find & Select** drop-down list in the **Editing** group on the **Home** tab, or by using the **Ctrl+F** shortcut key.

Advanced Search Options

Excel provides you with advanced options that allow you to search for specific information.

Option	Used To
The **Format** button	Search for formats. You can also click the drop-down arrow on this button to access the **Find Format** option.
The **Within** drop-down list	Restrict the search to either the active worksheet or the entire workbook.
The **Search** drop-down list	Specify whether the search should be performed by row or by column.
The **Look In** drop-down list	Specify whether the search target should include formulas, values, or comments.
The **Match Case** check box	Specify whether the search has to be for the text characters with the exact casing as specified in the search criteria.
The **Match Entire Cell Contents** check box	Specify whether the search has to be for the exact and complete characters that are specified in the search criteria.

The Replace Command

The **Replace** command allows you to replace any existing data in a workbook with new data. You can access this command from the **Find & Select** drop-down list in the **Editing** group on the **Home** tab or by using the **Ctrl+H** shortcut key. The **Replace** tab in the **Find and Replace** dialog box contains various options that allow you to select specific data and replace it.

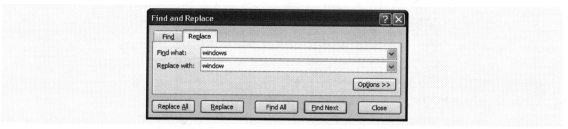

Figure 3-6: The Find and Replace dialog box with the Replace tab displayed.

The Spelling Dialog Box

The **Spelling** dialog box allows you to check for spelling and grammar errors in a workbook. The spell checker flags the text, such as proper words, numbers, dates, or time, that Excel does not recognize, as errors. The **Spelling** dialog box provides you with various options to use and customize the spell checker according to your requirements.

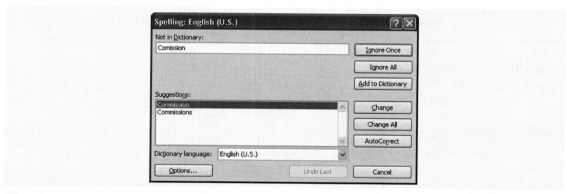

Figure 3-7: Word suggestions displayed in the Spelling dialog box.

Option	Description
Not in Dictionary	Displays the misspelled word that the spell checker identifies as an error.
Ignore Once	Ignores the current occurrence of the misspelled word.
Ignore All	Ignores all the occurrences of the misspelled word.
Add to Dictionary	Adds the misspelled word to the dictionary so that the spell checker recognizes the word as correct.
Suggestions	Lists all the possible correct spellings for the word that is displayed in the **Not in Dictionary** text box.
Change	Replaces the current occurrence of the misspelled word with the word selected in the **Suggestions** list box.

Option	Description
Change All	Replaces all the occurrences of the misspelled word with the word selected in the **Suggestions**list box.
Undo Last	Reverses the most recent action performed in the **Spelling** dialog box.
Options	Displays the **Excel Options** dialog box.
Dictionary Language	Provides options to select language for checking the text
AutoCorrect	Corrects all the occurrences of the misspelled word that is displayed in the **Not in Dictionary** text box. This will automatically correct the misspelled word across worksheets.

How to Find and Replace Data

Procedure Reference: Find and Replace Data in a Workbook

To find and replace cell data:

1. On the **Home** tab, in the **Editing** group, click **Find & Select,** and from the drop-down list, select **Replace.**

2. In the **Find and Replace** dialog box, on the **Replace** tab, in the **Find what** text box, type the search criteria.

3. In the **Replace with** text box, type the replacement data.

4. Click **Find Next** to find the next instance matching the search criteria.

 Click **Find All** to locate all the instances that match the search criteria and display a list of hyperlinks at the bottom of the **Find and Replace** dialog box. Click each hyperlink to make that cell active.

5. Click **Replace** to replace the selected instance that matches the search criteria with the replacement data.

 Click **Replace All** to replace all the instances that match the search criteria with the replacement data.

6. Repeat steps 4 and 5 until you have replaced the required data in the workbook.

7. Click **Close** to return to the worksheet.

Procedure Reference: Check a Worksheet for Spelling Errors

To check a worksheet for spelling errors:

1. On the **Review** tab, in the **Proofing** group, click **Spelling.**

2. In the **Spelling** dialog box, address the words that are flagged as misspelled words in the worksheet.

- Click **Ignore Once** to ignore the current instance of the misspelled word, or click **Ignore All** to overlook all the instances of the misspelled word.

- Click **Add to Dictionary** to add the misspelled word to the dictionary so that the spell checker recognizes the word as correct.

- In the **Suggestions** list box, select the correct word and click **Change** to replace the current occurrence of the misspelled word, or click **Change All** to replace all the occurrences of the misspelled word.

3. In the **Microsoft Excel** message box, click **OK** to acknowledge the completion of the spell-checking process.

ACTIVITY 3-2
Searching for Data in a Worksheet

Before You Begin:
The My Sales Report.xlsx file is open.

Scenario:
The Human Resources department has informed you of a name change for one of your team members. There is also a change in the region for two of your team members. You want to quickly locate the details of these employees in your worksheet and update the necessary information without having to scroll through the entire data.

---

1. Add cell names to specific cells.

    a. Select **Sheet1,** scroll to the right, and select cell **P3.**

    b. In the **Name Box,** click and type **Employees** and press **Enter** to name the cell.

    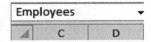

    c. Scroll to the left and select the cell range **A5:L5.**

    d. In the **Name Box,** click and type **Alice** and press **Enter** to name the cells.

---

2. Go to a named cell directly without scrolling.

    a. In the **Name Box,** click and type **Employees** and press **Enter** to go to cell P3 to view the cell that contains the employee total.

    b. Click the **Name Box** drop-down arrow, and from the displayed list, select **Alice.**

    c. Observe that the entire data of the employee, Alice, is selected whose range of cells were named earlier.

---

3. Update the region for the employee "Maureen."

    a. Select cell **A1.**

    b. On the **Home** tab, in the **Editing** group, from the **Find & Select** drop-down list, select **Find.**

c. In the **Find and Replace** dialog box, in the **Find what** text box, type *Maureen* and click **Find Next** and observe that the cell containing the name Maureen is selected.

d. Click **Close** to close the **Find and Replace** dialog box.

e. Select cell **B17,** type *Mideast* and press **Enter.**

4. Replace the employee name "Simon" with "Simone."

a. Select cell **A1,** and in the **Editing** group, from the **Find & Select** drop-down list, select **Replace.**

b. In the **Find and Replace** dialog box, in the **Find what** text box, double-click and type *Simon*

c. In the **Replace with** text box, click and type *Simone*

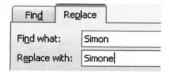

d. In the **Find and Replace** dialog box, click **Find Next.**

e. Click **Replace** to replace the text.

f. Click **Close** to close the **Find and Replace** dialog box.

g. Save the worksheet.

ACTIVITY 3-3
Checking a Worksheet for Spelling Errors

Before You Begin:
The My Sales Report.xlsx file is open.

Scenario:
Before you submit your sales report to the management, you want to ensure that the report is free of any spelling errors.

---

1. Display the **Spelling** dialog box.

    a. Select cell **A1,** and on the Ribbon, select the **Review** tab.

    b. In the **Proofing** group, click **Spelling** to display the **Spelling: English (U.S.)** dialog box.

    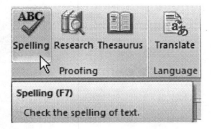

---

2. Correct the misspelled words across the worksheet.

    a. In the **Spelling: English (U.S.)** dialog box, in the **Not in Dictionary** text box, observe that the misspelled word is displayed. Also, observe that in the **Suggestions** list box, suggestions for the misspelled word are displayed.

    b. Click **Change** to change to the recommended word for "Commission."

    c. Observe that the next misspelled word is displayed in the **Not in Dictionary** text box, with a suggestion for the word in the **Suggestions** list box.

    d.   Click **Change** to replace "Southweet" with "Southwest."

    e.   In the **Microsoft Excel** message box, click **OK** to acknowledge the completion of the spell-checking process.

    f.   Save the worksheet.

TOPIC C
Manipulate Worksheet Elements

You proofed the worksheet data for any spelling errors. The data in some of the cells may exceed the default width of the cell resulting in poor readability of contents in the worksheet. You may need to alter the width of the cell to view such data easily. In this topic, you will adjust the width of columns and the height of rows.

It will be difficult to work with a worksheet where data you need to view is obscured within rows that are too short or columns that are too narrow. It also takes away the visual appeal of the worksheet. By changing the column width and row height, you can ensure that the data stored in the rows and columns will fit correctly within their respective cells.

The Insert and Delete Options

The **Insert** and **Delete** options in Excel allow you to insert or delete cells, columns, and rows. When you access the **Insert** command, the **Insert** dialog box is displayed providing you with options to insert a cell, row, or column, and shifting the consecutive cell to the right or down. When you access the **Delete** command, the **Delete** dialog box is displayed providing you with options to delete a cell, row, or column, and shifting the consecutive cell to the left or up.

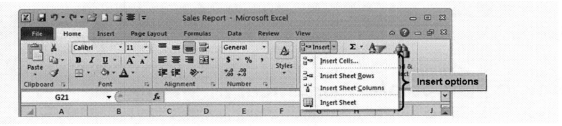

Figure 3-8: The Insert drop-down list.

Column Width and Row Height Alteration Methods

Excel provides you with several methods that you can use to adjust the column width and row height in a worksheet. These options include:

- Automatically adjusting the column width and row height using the **AutoFit** option.
- Manually adjusting the column width and row height to fit the content by dragging or by double-clicking the borders between two columns or rows.
- Setting a specific column width and row height using the options in the **Column Width** or **Row Height** dialog box.

Excel displays the hash (####) sign in cells when the numeric or date and time data is too wide to be displayed within the current column width. When the column width is adjusted, the hash (####) sign disappears and the numeric or date and time data is displayed.

The Hide and Unhide Options

The **Hide** option allows you to hide columns or rows in a worksheet, while the **Unhide** option allows you to unhide the hidden columns or rows. When rows and columns are hidden, they exist in the worksheet, but are not visible, until they are unhidden. The references to cells, columns, or rows that are hidden do not change.

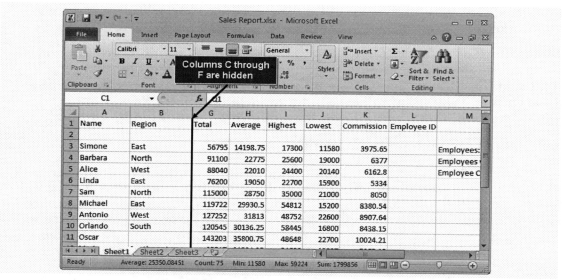

Figure 3-9: *A worksheet with hidden columns.*

How to Manipulate Worksheet Elements

Procedure Reference: Change the Column Width and Row Height

To change the column width and row height:

1. Change the column width.
   - Change the column width to a specific value.
     a. Select the column that you want to change.
        - Right-click the selection and choose **Column Width.**
        - On the **Home** tab, in the **Cells** group, from the **Format** drop-down list, under the **Cell Size** section, click **Column Width.**
     b. In the **Column Width** dialog box, in the **Column width** text box, type a new value for the column width.
     c. Click **OK** to change the column width.
   - In the column header, drag the column's right border to the left or right to adjust the column width manually.
   - In the column header, double-click the right border to automatically fit the overflowing text.

2. Change the row height.
   - Change the row height to a specific value.
     a. Select the row that you want to change.
        - Right-click the selection and choose **Row Height.**

- On the **Home** tab, in the **Cells** group, from the **Format** drop-down list, under the **Cell Size** section, click **Row Height.**

  b. In the **Row Height** dialog box, in the **Row height** text box, type a new value for the row height.

  c. Click **OK** to change the row height.

- In the row header, drag the upper border above or below to adjust the row width manually.

- In the row header, double-click the above border to automatically fit the overflowing text.

Procedure Reference: Insert or Delete Rows or Columns

To insert or delete rows or columns:

1. Select a row or column.
2. On the **Home** tab, in the **Cells** group, click **Insert** or **Delete.**

Procedure Reference: Insert or Delete a Range of Cells

To insert or delete a range of cells:

1. Select a range of cells.
2. On the **Home** tab, in the **Cells** group, from the **Insert or Delete** drop-down list, select **Insert Cells** or **Delete Cells.**
3. In the **Insert** or **Delete** dialog box, select the preferred option to shift cells up, down, left, or right and click **OK.**

Procedure Reference: Hide or Unhide Columns or Rows

To hide or unhide columns or rows:

1. Select the column or row that you want to hide or unhide.

 To select hidden rows or columns, select a range that includes the visible rows or columns on either side of the hidden rows or columns or type the desired range in the **Name Box.** You can also select multiple rows and columns to hide or unhide.

2. Hide the column or row.
   - On the **Home** tab, in the **Cells** group, from the **Format** drop-down list, from the **Hide & Unhide** submenu, select an option to hide the selected rows or columns.
     - Select **Hide Rows** to hide the selected rows or;
     - Select **Hide Columns** to hide the selected columns.
   - Right-click anywhere in the selected column or row and choose **Hide.**
3. If necessary, unhide the column or row.
   - On the **Home** tab, in the **Cells** group, from the **Format** drop-down list, from the **Hide & Unhide** submenu, select an option to unhide the selected rows or columns.
     - Select **Unhide Rows** to unhide the selected rows or;
     - Select **Unhide Columns** to unhide the selected columns.
   - Right-click anywhere in the selected column or row and choose **Unhide.**

ACTIVITY 3-4
Adjusting Columns

Before You Begin:

The My Sales Report file is open.

Scenario:

While reviewing the sales report, you realize that the column containing the details of employees name and region occupy more space than needed. Also, you want to hide the columns containing the details of quarterly results because you need only the employees total and average sales figures to make a judgement.

---

1. Adjust the width of columns A and B.

    a. Select column **A.**

    b. select the **Home** tab, and in the **Cells** group, click the **Format** drop-down arrow, and from the displayed list, select **AutoFit Column Width.**

    c. Double-click the border between columns B and C to adjust the contents in column B.

    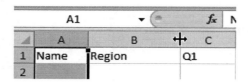

    d. Observe that the column width of columns A and B are adjusted to fit the contents in the cell.

---

2. Hide columns C, D, E, and F.

    a. Select column **C.**

    b. Hold down **Shift** and click column **F.**

    c. On the **Home** tab, in the **Cells** group, in the **Format** drop-down list, move the mouse pointer over **Hide & Unhide,** and from the submenu that is displayed, choose **Hide Columns.**

    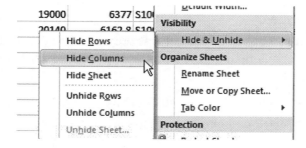

---

d.   Observe the column headings. Because the columns C through F are hidden, the worksheet displays column G after column B.

e.   In the **Cells** group, in the **Format** drop-down list, move the mouse pointer over **Hide & Unhide,** and from the submenu that is displayed, choose **Unhide Columns.**

f.   Save and close the worksheet.

Lesson 3 Follow-up

In this lesson, you modified an Excel worksheet. Modifying worksheets lets you update the existing data based on your requirements, rather than creating a new worksheet every time the data changes.

1. **What are the advantages of using the Find and Select options?**

2. **When will you use various data manipulation options such as Auto Fill, Undo, and Redo?**

4 | Modifying the Appearance of a Worksheet

Lesson Time: 1 hour(s)

Lesson Objectives:

In this lesson, you will modify the appearance of data within a worksheet.

You will:

- Apply font properties.
- Add borders and colors to cells.
- Align content in a cell.
- Apply number formatting.
- Apply cell styles.

Introduction

You modified data in a worksheet. You may now want to enhance the appearance of the worksheet by using certain formatting options, which will help you quickly differentiate the data in the worksheet. In this lesson, you will modify the appearance of the worksheet.

A worksheet that is not formatted properly will look cluttered and it will be difficult to analyze its data. By highlighting specific cells, rows, or columns and using other formatting methods, you can not only ensure that the required data stands apart, but also classify sets of data visually. With Excel, your formatted worksheets can help you analyze data and locate the desired information efficiently.

TOPIC A
Apply Font Properties

You modified the data in a worksheet. You now want to emphasize important data in the worksheet so that it is easy to locate necessary information and enhance the appearance of the worksheet. In this topic, you will apply font properties to data in an Excel worksheet.

Newspaper headlines are always larger and much more prominent from the text of the news stories. This is done to attract readers to a particular news item, and enables a reader to easily and quickly scan and locate important news stories. In a similar way, altering the font properties of the data in a worksheet helps you highlight key points from the rest of the data. By modifying the font properties, you can also change the appearance of the worksheet to make it look visually appealing.

Fonts

Definition:

A *font* is a predefined *typeface* that can be used for formatting characters. Each font has a unique style and character spacing. Fonts can be either built in or user defined. Typefaces can be letters, numbers, punctuation marks, symbols, and other graphical characters called ideograms.

Example:

Figure 4-1: *Various font faces.*

The Font Group

The **Font** group on the **Home** tab contains options to set font properties such as font face, size, and color. You can also access these options from the **Format Cells** dialog box.

Figure 4-2: *The Font group on the Home tab.*

The Format Cells Dialog Box

The **Format Cells** dialog box contains various options for formatting the appearance of data in an Excel worksheet. You can preview the format result in the preview section, before you apply it to the data. The **Format Cells** dialog box consists of six tabs containing formatting options.

Tab	Enables You To
Number	Specify the options for changing the number formatting such as **Currency, Short Date, Long Date,** and **Time.**
Alignment	Specify the options for changing the alignment and orientation of data in a cell range. It also contains options to wrap text and merge cells.
Font	Specify the font properties such as **Font Face, Style, Size,** and **Color.**
Border	Specify the border formatting options such as **Line** and **Color.**
Fill	Specify the fill color options such as **Background Color, Pattern Color,** and **Pattern Style.**
Protection	Specify the protection options such as locking cells or hiding formulas in a worksheet.

The Format Painter

The *format painter* provides you with an easy option to copy only the formatting that is applied to a cell to another cell or cell range, without copying the data. The format painter works similar to a paintbrush and can be used to apply format changes to data, or to copy a color scheme from one cell to another. When you select the format painter, the cursor includes a paint brush graphic. You can double-click the **Format Painter** button to apply the same formatting to multiple cells in a worksheet.

Galleries

A *gallery* is a repository for elements that belong to the same category. In Excel, a gallery acts as a central location for accessing various preset styles and appearance settings for an object. Excel provides galleries for various options such as cell styles, tables, shapes, and charts. Galleries enable you to choose from any of the preset formats and styles to quickly alter worksheet objects.

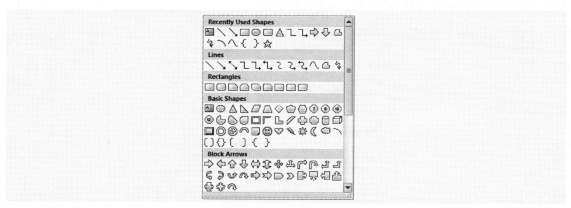

Figure 4-3: *A gallery providing various options for shapes.*

The Mini Toolbar

The *Mini toolbar* is a floating toolbar that is displayed when you right-click a cell or select data within a cell. It combines some of the options available in the various groups on the **Home** tab, and provides easy and quick access to some of the frequently used formatting options. This toolbar is automatically displayed when data is selected within a cell and remains semi-transparent until the mouse pointer is hovered over it. Although the Mini toolbar is not customizable, you can turn it off.

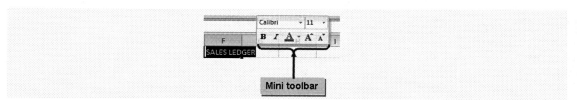

Figure 4-4: *The Mini toolbar displayed when text in a cell is selected.*

How to Apply Font Properties

Procedure Reference: Change the Font Face, Size, Color, and Style Using the Font Group

To change the font face, size, color, and style using the **Font** group:

1. Select the cell that contains the data you want to format.
2. On the **Home** tab, in the **Font** group, change the font properties.
    *   From the **Font** drop-down list, select the desired font face.
    *   Change the font size.
        *   From the **Font Size** drop-down list, select the desired font size.
        *   Click the **Increase Font Size** or **Decrease Font Size** button.
    *   From the **Font Color** drop-down list, select the desired color.
    *   If necessary, click the **Bold, Italic,** and **Underline** buttons to apply the respective formatting.

 You can also right-click the cell that contains the data you want to format, and on the Mini toolbar, select the desired font face, size, color, and style.

Procedure Reference: Change the Font Properties Using the Format Cells Dialog Box

To change the font properties using the **Format Cells** dialog box:

1. Display the **Format Cells** dialog box.
    *   On the **Home** tab, in the **Font** group, click the **Font** dialog box launcher or;
    *   On the **Home** tab, in the **Cells** group, click the **Format** drop-down arrow and select **Format Cells.**
2. In the **Format Cells** dialog box, on the **Font** tab, change the font properties.
    *   In the **Font** list box, select the desired font.
    *   In the **Font Style** list box, select the desired font style.
    *   In the **Size** list box, select the desired font size, or enter a value in the **Size** text box.
    *   Click the **Underline** drop-down arrow and from the displayed list, select an underline style.
    *   From the **Font Color** drop-down list, select the desired color.
    *   Change the font effects.
        *   Check the **Strikethrough** check box to strike through the text.
        *   Check the **Superscript** check box to make the text superscript.
        *   Check the **Subscript** check box to make the text subscript.
3. In the **Preview** section, preview the font properties and click **OK** to apply the changes.

Procedure Reference: Format Cells Using the Format Painter

To format cells using the format painter:

1. Click a cell with the formatting that you want to copy.

2.   Apply the formatting to a different cell.

    a.   On the **Home** tab, in the **Clipboard** group, click **Format Painter.**

 Observe that the mouse pointer includes a paint brush graphic.

    b.   Move to the cell where you want to apply the formatting and click on it.

3.   Apply the formatting to multiple cells.

- Double-click **Format Painter** and then click multiple individual cells to apply the format or;
- Click and drag across a group of cells.

4.   Click **Format Painter** again, or press **Esc** to turn off the format painter.

ACTIVITY 4-1
Modifying Fonts

Data Files:

C:\084576Data\Modifying the Appearance of a Worksheet\Sales Ledger Final.xlsx

Scenario:

You are preparing a sales report for the period Q1 to Q3. You feel that you need to make the worksheet look more visually appealing. Therefore, you decide to modify the font properties of the data in the worksheet.

---

1. Change the font face of the data in the entire worksheet.

    a. Navigate to the C:\084576Data\Modifying the Appearance of a Worksheet folder and open the Sales Ledger Final.xlsx file.

    b. Click the Select All button, ▢ to select the entire worksheet.

    c. On the **Home** tab, in the **Font** group, click the **Font** drop-down arrow, and in the displayed list, scroll down and select **Times New Roman.**

    d. Observe that the font for the entire worksheet has changed to Times New Roman.

---

2. Format the worksheet title.

    a. Select cell **F1.**

    b. On the **Home** tab, in the **Font** group, click the **Font Size** drop-down arrow and from the displayed list, select **18.**

    c. In the **Font** group, click the **Bold** button. **B**

    d. Observe that the worksheet title is formatted.

---

3. Format the other headings and names in the worksheet.

    a. Select the cell range **A2:I2.**

    b. From the **Font Size** drop-down list, select **12** to increase the size of the selected headings.

    c. In the **Font** group, click the **Bold** button.

    d. Select the cell range **A4:A26.**

    e. On the **Home** tab, in the **Font** group, click the **Increase Font Size** button which is the first button after the **Font Size** drop-down list. $\boxed{\text{A}^{\cdot}}$

    f. Scroll up and in the header row, double-click the right edge of Column I to automatically adjust the width of column I to fit the heading "Commission."

    g. Save the worksheet as *My Sales Ledger Final*

TOPIC B
Add Borders and Colors to Cells

You modified the fonts of data in a worksheet to emphasize specific data. After emphasizing specific data, you may want to highlight key information in the worksheet by using various borders and colors. In this topic, you will add borders and colors to cells.

Billboard advertisements are designed to catch a person's attention. Successful advertisements highlight the key information to attract the attention of the passerby. Similarly, adding borders and colors to specific cells in a worksheet helps you highlight key information. It also allows the grouping of similar data and makes worksheets that have loads of data look uncluttered. Excel provides you with various options for adding borders and colors to cells.

Borders

Borders enable you to emphasize and define sections in a worksheet. In Excel, you can apply borders to the sides of a cell or a range of cells in a worksheet. You can specify a border style or color that you want to apply to the selected cells in a worksheet. You can also remove any borders that are applied to cells if you do not require them.

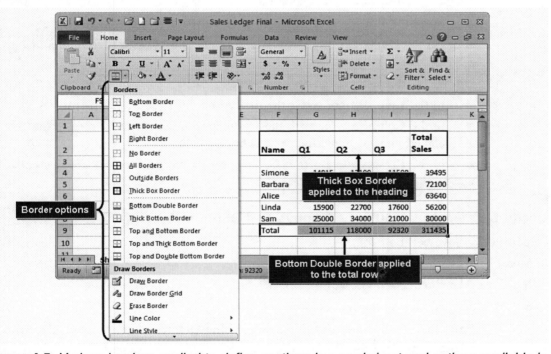

Figure 4-5: *Various borders applied to define sections in a worksheet and options available in the Border drop-down list.*

Fills

Fills are worksheet enhancements that allow you to add background colors and highlight specific cells to draw attention to important data. You can choose from standard colors, define a custom color, or set a desired background effect. You can also select from a list of patterns and pattern colors to apply to the selected cells in a worksheet.

How to Add Borders and Colors to Cells

Procedure Reference: Add Borders to Cells

To add borders to cells:

1.   Select the cells to which you need to add borders.

2.   Apply a border to the selected cells.

-   On the **Home** tab, in the **Font** group, click the **Border** drop-down arrow, and from the displayed list, select the desired border or;

-   Right-click the selected cells, and on the displayed Mini toolbar, click the **Border** drop-down arrow, and from the displayed list, select the desired border or;

-   Select the desired option from the **Format Cells** dialog box.

    a.   Display the **Format Cells** dialog box.

    -   From the **Border** drop-down list, select **More Borders** or;

    -   On the **Home** tab, in the **Cells** group, click the **Format** button, and from the displayed list, select **Format Cells.**

    b.   On the **Border** tab, set the desired border.

    -   In the **Line** section, select the desired border style.

    -   In the **Color** section, click the **Color** drop-down arrow, and from the displayed gallery, select the desired border color.

    -   In the **Presets** and **Border** sections, set the borders for the selected cells.

    c.   Preview the border and click **OK.**

Procedure Reference: Modify or Remove Cell Borders

To modify or remove cell borders:

1.   Modify the cell borders.

-   From the **Border** drop-down list, select a border.

-   If necessary, change the line color of a border.

    a.   From the **Border** drop-down list, select **Line Color,** and from the displayed gallery, select a desired color.

 The mouse pointer will be displayed as a pencil graphic.

    b.   Select the lines to which you want to apply the color.

    c.   Click the **Border** button, or press **Esc** to change to the normal mouse pointer.

-   If necessary, change the line style of a border.

    a.   From the **Border** drop-down list, select **Line Style,** and from the displayed gallery, select a desired style.

 Observe that the mouse pointer has changed to a pencil graphic.

    b.   Select the lines to which you want to apply the style.

    c.   Click the **Border** button, or press **Esc** to change to the normal mouse pointer.

2.   In the worksheet, select the cells from which you need to remove the borders.

3.   Remove the borders.

- On the **Home** tab, in the **Font** group, click the **Border** drop-down arrow, and from the displayed list, select **No Border** or;

- Display the **Format Cells** dialog box, select the **Border** tab, and in the **Presets** section, select **None** and click **OK** or;

- Right-click the selected cells, and on the displayed Mini toolbar, click the **Border** drop-down arrow, and from the displayed list, select **No Border.**

Procedure Reference: Add a Color to Cells

To add a color to cells:

1.   Select the desired cells to which you want to add a color.

2.   Apply the desired color.

- On the **Home** tab, in the **Font** group, click the **Fill Color** drop-down arrow, and from the displayed gallery, select the desired color or;

- Right-click the selected cells, and on the displayed Mini toolbar, click the **Fill Color** drop-down arrow, and from the displayed gallery, select the desired color or;

- In the **Format Cells** dialog box, select the **Fill** tab, select a color, and click **OK.**

    - In the **Background Color** section, select the desired color.

    - Click the **Pattern Color** drop-down arrow, and from the displayed gallery, select the desired color.

    - Click the **Pattern Style** drop-down arrow, and from the displayed gallery, select the desired pattern.

 Selecting the **No Color** option will remove the color applied to the selected cell or cell range.

ACTIVITY 4-2
Adding Borders and Colors to Cells

Before You Begin:
The My Sales Ledger Final.xlsx file is open.

Scenario:
You are still in the process of formatting the sales analysis report that you need to present to the management. You want to highlight the title and heading of the data in the worksheet. You also want to add an outline to the data cells in the worksheet.

1. Add a background color to the worksheet title and headings.

    a. Select the cell range **A1:I1.**

    b. On the **Home** tab, in the **Font** group, click the **Fill Color** drop-down arrow, and from the displayed gallery, in the **Theme Colors** section, select **Blue, Accent 1, Darker 25%** which is the fifth color in the fifth row.

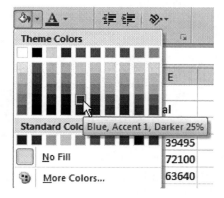

    c. Select the cell range **A2:I2.**

    d. On the **Home** tab, in the **Font** group, click the **Fill Color** drop-down arrow, and from the displayed gallery, in the **Theme Colors** section, select **Aqua, Accent 5, Lighter 40%,** which is the ninth color in the fourth row.

2. Add a border to the A2:I26 cell range.

    a. Verify that the cell range A2:I2 is selected.

    b. On the **Home** tab, in the **Clipboard** group, click the **Format Painter** button, ✏️ and select cell **K12** and drag it till cell L16.

    c. Select the cell range **A2:I26.**

d. On the **Home** tab, in the **Font** group, click the **Border** drop-down arrow, and from the displayed list, select **All Borders.**

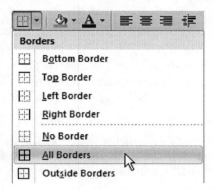

e. Click any cell to deselect the highlighted region.

f. Save the worksheet.

TOPIC C
Align Content in a Cell

You added borders and colors to the cells in a worksheet to enhance the look of the worksheet. By positioning the data in the cells, you can enhance the readability and comprehension of the content presented in a worksheet. In this topic, you will align the content within a cell.

When you enter data in a cell, Excel may not align the content within the cell as you wanted. Sometimes, when the data exceeds the column width, some part of the data will not be visible within the cells. Aligning the content within a cell improves the appearance of the worksheet content. Excel provides you with various options that enable you to align content within a cell.

Alignment Options

The **Alignment** options in Excel enable you to align content within a cell either horizontally or vertically. These options can be accessed from the **Alignment** group on the **Home** tab.

Alignment Option	Used To
Top Align	Align text to the top of a cell.
Middle Align	Align text to the vertical center of a cell.
Bottom Align	Align text to the bottom of a cell.
Align Text Left	Align text to the left of a cell.
Center	Align text to the horizontal center of a cell.
Align Text Right	Align text to the right of a cell.

The Indent Command

The *Indent* command is used to reposition data in cells for better spacing and readability. The **Decrease Indent** command decreases the space between the left border and the text within a cell. The **Increase Indent** command increases the space between the left border and the text within a cell.

Figure 4-6: *The two Indent commands used to reposition the data in a cell.*

The Wrap Text Option

Excel enables you to automatically wrap the text within a cell by using the **Wrap Text** option. If the text within a cell extends beyond the space available, this option moves the content to the next line within the cell and automatically modifies the row height to ensure that all of the text is visible within the cell.

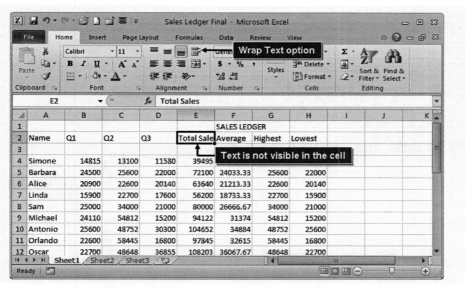

Figure 4-7: Text exceeding the space within a cell.

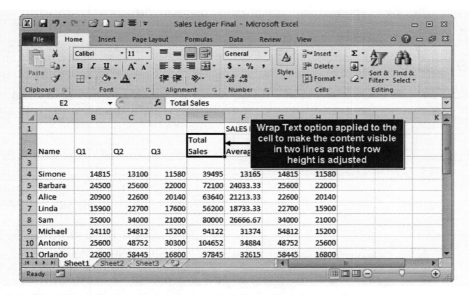

Figure 4-8: The Wrap Text option used to fit the content in a cell.

Manual Line Breaks

The content in a cell can be wrapped within a cell by entering a manual line break. After locating the point at which the line needs to be broken, a manual line break can be inserted by holding down **Alt** and pressing **Enter.**

Orientation Options

To display data in a worksheet legibly and with some symmetry, you may have to change the orientation of data in cells. Often, when the column header text is longer than the data contained below it, you may want to change the angle of the header text diagonally or vertically to minimize the column width. This allows you to fit more columns on a page. The orientation options are usually used for labeling narrow columns. Excel allows you to orient data clockwise, counterclockwise, vertically, or by a specific degree.

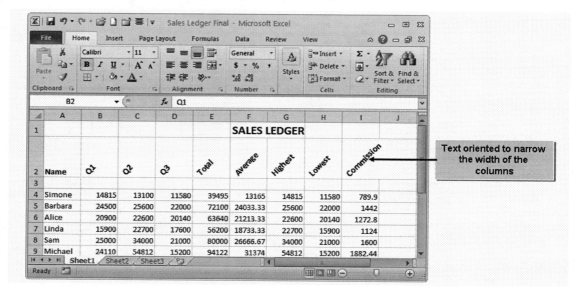

Figure 4-9: *The Orientation option used to change the angle of the text.*

The Merge Feature

Excel provides you with options to not only merge contiguous cells across columns and rows, but also split cells that are merged.

Merge Option	Description
Merge & Center	Combines the selected cells across columns and rows to a larger, single cell and centers the data. Only the data in the top-left cell that is merged will be retained.
Merge Across	Combines the selected cells across columns to a larger, single cell. When multiple rows of data are selected, the cells are merged across columns for each row separately. Only the data in the first cell from the left of each row that is merged will be retained.
Merge Cells	Combines the selected cells across columns and rows to a larger, single cell. Only the data in the top-left cell will be retained.
Unmerge Cells	Splits the merged cell into separate cells. The data of the merged cell is copied only to the top-left cell that was separated.

How to Align Content in a Cell

Procedure Reference: Align Content in a Cell

To align content in a cell:

1. Select the cell in which you want to align the content.

2. Align the content of the selected cell.

   - On the **Home** tab, in the **Alignment** group, select the desired option to align the text within the cell or;

   - Display the **Format Cells** dialog box, and on the **Alignment** tab, in the **Text Alignment** section, click either the **Horizontal** or the **Vertical** drop-down arrow, and from the displayed list, select an option or;

   - Right-click the selected cell, and on the displayed Mini toolbar, click the **Center** button to align the content to the center.

3. Indent the content in a cell.

   a. Select the cell in which you want to indent the content.

   b. Indent the content of the selected cell.

      - On the **Home** tab, in the **Alignment** group, click the **Increase Indent** or **Decrease Indent** button to increase or decrease the indent between the border and text within a cell or;

      - In the **Format Cells** dialog box, on the **Alignment** tab, in the **Indent** section, enter a value, or click the up or down arrow to specify an indent value in the spin box.

4. If necessary, orient the content in a cell.

   a. Select the cell in which you want to orient the content.

   b. Orient the content in the selected cell.

      - Click the **Orientation** button, and from the displayed list, select the desired option.

        - Select **Angle Counterclockwise** to rotate the text in a cell selection up 45 degrees from the baseline.

        - Select **Angle Clockwise** to rotate the text in a cell selection down 45 degrees from the baseline.

        - Select **Vertical Text** to align the text in a column where one letter appears over the other.

        - Select **Rotate Text Up** to rotate the text in a cell selection up 90 degrees from the baseline.

        - Select **Rotate Text Down** to rotate the text in a cell selection down 90 degrees from the baseline.

      - Orient the content in a cell using the **Format Cells** dialog box.

        A. In the **Format Cells** dialog box, on the **Alignment** tab, in the **Orientation** section, enter a value or click the up or down arrow to specify a degree in the spin box.

        B. Preview the text in the place provided above the spin box.

Procedure Reference: Wrap Text in a Cell

To wrap text in a cell:

1. Select the cells in which the text needs to be wrapped.

2. Wrap the text in the selected cells.

    *   On the **Home** tab, in the **Alignment** group, click **Wrap Text** or;

    *   Display the **Format Cells** dialog box, select the **Alignment** tab, check the **Wrap text** check box, and click **OK** or;

    *   If necessary, in the **Format Cells** dialog box, on the **Alignment** tab, in the **Text Control** section, check the **Shrink to fit** check box to shrink the text to be visible within the cell.

Procedure Reference: Merge or Split Cells

To merge or split cells:

1. Select the range of contiguous cells that you want to merge or a merged cell that you want to split.

2. Merge or split the selected cells.

    *   Display the **Format Cells** dialog box, select the **Alignment** tab, and in the **Text control** section, check or uncheck the **Merge cells** check box and click **OK** or;

    *   Right-click the selected range of cells, and on the displayed Mini toolbar, click the **Merge & Center** button or;

    *   On the **Home** tab, in the **Alignment** group, click the **Merge & Center** drop-down arrow, and from the displayed list, select the desired option.

ACTIVITY 4-3
Positioning the Content in a Cell

Before You Begin:
The My Sales Ledger Final.xlsx file is open.

Scenario:
You reviewed the sales report and noticed that the headings in the worksheet are not aligned with the data. You also observed that the text in some of the cells exceeds the available space and is not displayed completely. You want to align the cell content to enhance the readability of the worksheet's contents.

---

1. Align the text in the cell range B2:I2 to the right.

   a. Select the cell range **B2:I2**.

   b. On the **Home** tab, in the **Alignment** group, click the **Align Text Right** button, to right align the content in the cells.

---

2. Merge and center the title "Sales Ledger."

   a. Select the cell range **A1:I1**.

   b. On the **Home** tab, in the **Alignment** group, click the **Merge & Center** button.

   c. Double-click the border between the rows 1 and 2 to automatically adjust the height of row 1.

   d. Observe that the title "Sales Ledger" is displayed at the center of a single large cell.

---

3. Wrap the text "Commission rate" to fit in a single cell.

   a. Select cell **K3**.

   b. Observe that some of the content displayed on the Formula Bar does not appear in the cell because the space available in the cell is not sufficient to display the full content.

   c. On the **Home** tab, in the **Alignment** group, click the **Wrap Text** button.

   d. Observe that the text "Commission rate" now fits in a single cell.

   > Commission
   > rate:

   e. Save the worksheet.

TOPIC D
Apply Number Formatting

You aligned content in cells to improve the presentation of data in a worksheet. When you have numerical data in a worksheet, you may want this data to appear in specific formats so that you can interpret it easily. In this topic, you will apply number formats.

When creating spreadsheets, you may have specific requirements to present data in a particular cell, row, or column. If you are working on an inventory worksheet that contains a column for the stock's value, you may need to manually enter the currency symbol for each cell. Excel provides you with various number formats that can be applied to such cells so that the value displayed in the cells are formatted automatically. Applying number formats changes the appearance of the numerical data and makes it easier to understand the data present in the cells.

Data Formats in Excel

A data format changes the appearance of the data in a cell by applying specialized formatting to the data. Applying data format changes only the appearance of the data, but not the actual data. You can apply the desired format to a cell or a range of cells before or after you enter data. Excel provides you with a variety of data format categories.

Category	*Used To*
General	Display data using the default formatting that Excel applies when you enter data in a cell.
Number	Display numbers. You can specify the number of decimal places and the format in which the negative numbers will be displayed.
Currency	Display monetary values. The currency symbol is displayed in a cell along with the value. By default, the dollar ($) sign is displayed. You can also change the sign to the currency sign that you need.
Accounting	Display monetary values with decimals. This will align the currency symbols and decimal points of the numbers in a column.
Date	Display date or a combination of date and time values according to the type and location that you specify.
Time	Display time or a combination of time and date values according to the type and location that you specify.
Percentage	Display percentages by multiplying the cell value by 100 and displaying the result with a percent symbol.
Fraction	Display a fraction according to the type of fraction that you specify.
Scientific	Display an exponential notation.
Text	Display text. Even when a cell contains numbers, you can use this option to treat the content as text so that the numbers appear exactly the same as you type them. You can use this option when leading zeros are necessary, as in an employee number.
Special	Display data with special formatting such as ZIP code, phone number, or Social Security Number.

Category	Used To
Custom	Create a custom format. You can also customize an existing format.

Custom Data Formats

Excel allows you to create custom data formats to suit your needs. Custom data formats can be created when Excel's predefined format categories do not provide the format that is required for a particular type of data. When creating a custom data format, the # symbol is used to indicate that only significant digits will be displayed, while the insignificant zeros will not be displayed. Quotation marks at the beginning and end of the text are used to indicate how the text should be displayed with the custom data format. You can add up to 250 custom data formats to a list.

How to Apply Number Formatting

Procedure Reference: Apply Number Formats

To apply number formats:

1. Select the cell to which you want to apply a number format.

2. Select the number format.

   - On the **Home** tab, in the **Number** group, click the **Number Format** drop-down arrow, and from the displayed list, select the desired number format or;

   - Display the **Format Cells** dialog box, select the **Number** tab, and in the **Category** list box, select the desired number format.

Procedure Reference: Create a Custom Number Format

To create a custom number format:

1. Select the cell to which you want to apply a custom number format.

2. Display the **Format Cells** dialog box and select the **Number** tab.

3. In the **Category** list box, select **Custom.**

4. Define the new custom format.

   - In the **Type** text box, type the desired format using one of the existing formats as the starting point to define a new custom format or;

   - In the **Type** list box, select one of the existing models and modify it in the **Type** text box.

5. Click **OK** to apply the format.

ACTIVITY 4-4
Applying a Number Format

Before You Begin:
The My Sales Ledger Final.xlsx file is open.

Scenario:
When checking the sales report for accuracy, you notice that it contains a lot of numerical information. You find it difficult to interpret this data because it is not formatted properly and decide to apply appropriate formatting.

1. Apply a currency format to the sales data and the top three employees' summary.

 If you use the **Currency** button in the **Number** group, it applies the **Accounting** number format, which requires a wider column.

    a. Select the cell range **B4:I26.**

    b. Hold down **Ctrl** and click cell **L14.**

    c. Hold down **Shift** and click cell **L16.**

    d. On the **Home** tab, in the **Number** group, from the **Number Format** drop-down list, select **Currency** to apply the currency format to the selected range with the dollar sign.

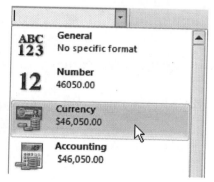

 The ## sign will appear if the column is not wide enough to display the numbers with the currency format.

    e. Click the **Decrease Decimal** button, [icon] twice to display the values without decimal points.

2. Enter the date and change its format.

a. In the **Name Box,** click and type *L1* and press **Enter** to navigate to cell L1.

b. Type the current date and press **Enter.**

c. Observe that the date in the cell L1 is displayed in the dd-mmm format.

d. Select cell **L1.**

e. On the **Home** tab, in the **Number** group, click the **Format Cells: Number** dialog box launcher.

f. On the **Number** tab, in the **Category** list box, select **Date.**

g. In the **Type** list box, scroll down and select **14-Mar-2001** and click **OK** to apply this date format to the selected cell.

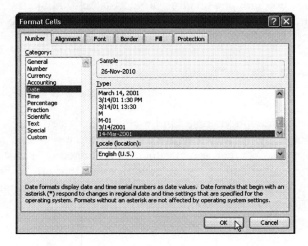

h. Observe that the date is displayed in the dd-mmm-yyyy format.

i. Save the worksheet.

TOPIC E
Apply Cell Styles

You applied number formats to display data in a worksheet in the preferred format. Applying a cell style gives you a way to create consistent-looking documents and also gives the ability to change the formatting of all the cells that use a particular style. In this topic, you will apply cell styles in a worksheet.

While creating a worksheet, you notice that some of the similar cells are formatted differently. This results in an inconsistent look of the spreadsheet. Ensuring that the different formatting options such as the font style, font size, borders, and shading are consistently applied throughout the workbook can be a time-consuming task. Excel provides you with cell styles to apply several formatting options to similar cells at the same time for a neat and consistent look.

Cell Styles

Definition:

A *cell style* is a predefined set of appearance options that can be applied to a cell in a worksheet. Each style includes a unique combination of number formatting, alignment, font, border style, pattern, and protection options. You can select either a predefined or a customized cell style to suit your requirements. Predefined cell styles are sets of styles that are based on the theme of the workbook template. You can lock a cell style to prevent others from modifying it. You can also delete cell styles that you no longer require.

Example:

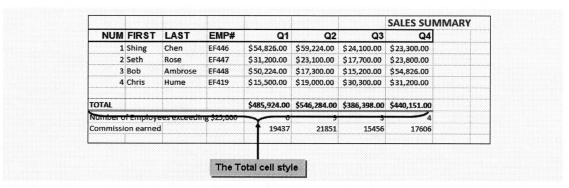

	NUM	FIRST	LAST	EMP#	Q1	Q2	Q3	Q4	SALES SUMMARY
	1	Shing	Chen	EF446	$54,826.00	$59,224.00	$24,100.00	$23,300.00	
	2	Seth	Rose	EF447	$31,200.00	$23,100.00	$17,700.00	$23,800.00	
	3	Bob	Ambrose	EF448	$50,224.00	$17,300.00	$15,200.00	$54,826.00	
	4	Chris	Hume	EF419	$15,500.00	$19,000.00	$30,300.00	$31,200.00	
TOTAL					$485,924.00	$546,284.00	$386,398.00	$440,151.00	
Number of Employees exceeding $25,000					6	5	5	4	
Commission earned					19437	21851	15456	17606	

The Total cell style

Figure 4-10: The Total cell style used to differentiate the total values in a worksheet.

The Style Dialog Box

The **Style** dialog box contains various options that allow you to modify an existing cell style or create a new cell style. This dialog box can be accessed from the gallery that is displayed on clicking the **Cell Styles** button in the **Styles** group on the **Home** tab. You can modify an existing cell style by selecting the **Modify** option in the list that is displayed when you right-click a cell style in the gallery. You can create a new cell style by selecting the **New Cell Style** option from the gallery. The modified or newly created cell style will also be listed in the gallery.

The **Style** dialog box contains various options to customize cell styles.

Option	Used To
The **Style Name** text box	Specify the name of the style that you want to modify.
The **Format** button	Display the **Format Cells** dialog box. You can use this dialog box to modify the formatting used in the selected style.
The **Style Includes** section	Specify the formatting options that need to be included in the style. You can check the **Number, Alignment, Font, Border Fill,** and **Protection** check boxes to specify whether these formatting options are to be included in the style.

How to Apply Cell Styles

Procedure Reference: Apply a Cell Style

To apply a cell style:

1. Select the range of cells to which you want to apply a cell style.
2. On the **Home** tab, in the **Styles** group, click **Cell Styles.**
3. From the displayed gallery, select the desired cell style.

Procedure Reference: Modify a Cell Style

To modify a cell style:

1. On the **Home** tab, in the **Styles** group, click **Cell Styles,** and in the displayed gallery, right-click the desired cell style and choose **Modify.**
2. In the **Style** dialog box, click **Format.**
3. In the **Format Cells** dialog box, specify the modifications that need to be made to the cell style and click **OK.**
4. In the **Style** dialog box, in the **Style includes** section, specify the changes that need to be made to the cell style.
5. Click **OK** to apply the changes to the cell style.

 When you apply a cell style to the cells in a worksheet and then modify that cell style, the worksheet automatically reflects the modified cell style, without having to apply it again.

ACTIVITY 4-5
Applying Cell Styles

Before You Begin:
The My Sales Ledger Final.xlsx file is open.

Scenario:
When viewing the worksheet, you see that some cells containing similar data are not formatted uniformly. You decide to use the cell styles feature to apply the formatting that looks consistent across the worksheet. You also want to create a custom style that can be used for formatting titles on all official worksheets.

---

1. Apply a cell style to the worksheet title.

    a. Select the cell containing the title "Sales Ledger."

    b. On the **Home** tab, in the **Styles** group, click **Cell Styles,** and from the displayed gallery, in the **Titles and Headings** section, select **Title.**

    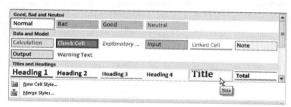

    c. Observe the cell style that is applied to the title.

---

2. Modify the font color of the applied cell style.

    a. In the **Styles** group, click **Cell Styles,** and in the displayed gallery, in the **Titles and Headings** section, right-click **Title** and choose **Modify.**

    b. In the **Style** dialog box, click **Format.**

    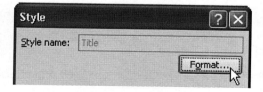

    c. In the **Format Cells** dialog box, select the **Font** tab.

d. On the **Font** tab, click the **Color** drop-down arrow, and from the displayed gallery, in the **Theme Colors** section, select **White, Background 1** which is the first color in the first row.

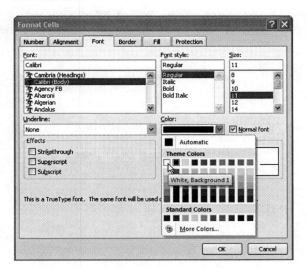

e. Click **OK** to close the **Format Cells** dialog box.

f. In the **Style** dialog box, observe that the **Font** check box is checked with the font properties displayed.

g. Click **OK** to apply the **Title** cell style.

3. Apply the **Accent5** theme style to the **Name** column.

a. Select the cell range **A4:A26.**

b. In the **Styles** group, click **Cell Styles,** and in the **Themed Cell Styles** section, select **Accent5.**

4. Apply the **Input** style to the cells that contain the data for the sales ledger.

a. Select the cell range **B4:D26.**

b. In the **Styles** group, click **Cell Styles,** and in the **Data and Model** section, select **Input.**

5. Apply the **Calculation** style to the cells that contain calculations.

a. Select the cell range **E4:I26.**

b. In the **Styles** group, click **Cell Styles,** and in the **Data and Model** section, select **Calculation.**

c. Click any cell to deselect the selected range.

d. Save and close the workbook.

Lesson 4 Follow-up

In this lesson, you modified the appearance of data in a worksheet. By applying the formatting options available in Excel, you can ensure that the worksheet looks professional and the data is easy to interpret.

1.   Why do you want to format a worksheet?

2.   Which formatting options do you think you will use the most often?

5 | Managing an Excel Workbook

Lesson Time: 1 hour(s)

Lesson Objectives:

In this lesson, you will manage Excel workbooks.

You will:

- Manage worksheets.
- View worksheets and workbooks.

Introduction

You modified the appearance of a worksheet. When working with multiple worksheets, you may need to organize them in an easily accessible way. In this lesson, you will manage workbooks.

Large workbooks have many unique issues that not only come into play, but also need to be managed. These workbooks may contain many worksheets with different sets of data. Also, individual worksheets may need to be rearranged, or you may need to compare and work with data located in distant sections of a worksheet. With the relevant knowledge of Excel's tools, you can efficiently manage and work with large workbooks.

TOPIC A
Manage Worksheets

You modified the appearance of a worksheet in a workbook. When a workbook contains multiple worksheets, you may spend a considerable amount of time in identifying the required worksheet. In this topic, you will manage the worksheets within a workbook.

Assume that you have entered data in different worksheets of a workbook based on regional sales information. Later, you realize that these worksheets are not sequenced properly, and you do not require some of the worksheets. Excel provides you with options to reposition, hide, or delete worksheets easily in a workbook.

Insertion and Deletion Options

When you open a new Excel workbook, three worksheets will be displayed on the sheet tab bar by default. Excel provides you with various options to modify the number of worksheets in a workbook based on your requirements. You can insert new worksheets by clicking the **Insert Worksheet** button, or by selecting the **Insert Sheet** option from the **Insert** drop-down list in the **Cells** group. You can also use the **Insert** dialog box to insert a blank worksheet, a worksheet based on a local template, or a worksheet based on a template from Office Online.

To delete worksheets with unwanted or obsolete data, you can select the **Delete Sheet** option from the **Delete** drop-down list in the **Cells** group, or choose **Delete** from the worksheet tab's shortcut menu.

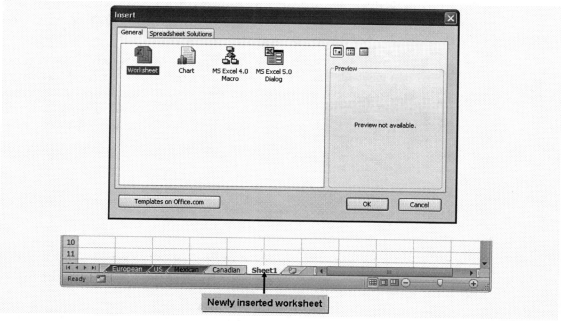

Figure 5-1: The Insert dialog box and a newly inserted worksheet.

Worksheet Repositioning Methods

Worksheet repositioning methods in Excel allow you to move or copy worksheets within a workbook or between workbooks. You can reposition worksheets by using the **Move or Copy** dialog box, or by dragging a worksheet tab to its new location.

Tab Formatting Options

Excel allows you to rename and change the color of worksheet tabs. You can change the default sheet names to something more meaningful so that you can locate appropriate data quickly. You can also change the color of a worksheet tab to enable easy identification of the worksheet.

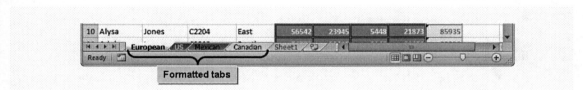

Figure 5-2: Formatting options available in the Format drop-down list.

Hide and Unhide Options

A workbook window may look cluttered when it contains multiple worksheets. In Excel, you can hide worksheets that are not required for a task in progress. The hidden worksheets are not deleted from the workbook and the references used in formulas to cells in a hidden worksheet are valid. The **Hide & Unhide** submenu of the **Format** menu in the **Cells** group provides you with the option to hide or display a worksheet. You can also hide or unhide a sheet by choosing an option from the worksheet tab's shortcut menu.

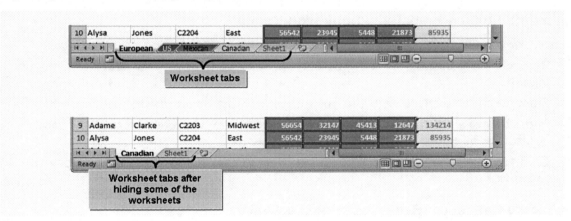

Figure 5-3: Hidden worksheets.

How to Manage Worksheets

Procedure Reference: Insert or Delete Worksheets

To insert or delete worksheets:

1. Insert new worksheets.

    - Insert a single worksheet.

        - Right-click the worksheet tab to the left of which the new worksheet needs to be added, choose **Insert,** and in the **Insert** dialog box, select the **Worksheet** option, and click **OK** or;

        - On the sheet tab bar, to the right of the worksheet tabs, click the **Insert Worksheet** button to insert a new worksheet or;

        - On the **Home** tab, in the **Cells** group, click the **Insert** drop-down arrow and select **Insert Sheet.**

    - Insert multiple worksheets.

        - On the sheet tab bar, select multiple worksheet tabs, and right-click the selection to the left of which the new worksheet needs to be added, choose **Insert,** and in the **Insert** dialog box, click **OK** or;

        - On the sheet tab bar, select multiple worksheet tabs, and on the **Home** tab, in the **Cells** group, click the **Insert** drop-down arrow and select **Insert Sheet** to insert multiple worksheets.

2. If necessary delete a worksheet.

    - Right-click a worksheet or a selection of multiple worksheets and choose **Delete** to delete worksheets.

    - Select a sheet or select multiple sheets, and on the **Home** tab in **Cells** group, from the **Delete** drop-down list, choose **Delete Sheet.**

Procedure Reference: Move or Copy Worksheets

To move or copy worksheets within a workbook or between workbooks:

1. Right-click a worksheet tab and choose **Move or Copy** to display the **Move or Copy** dialog box.

2. From the **Move selected sheets to book** drop-down list, select the destination workbook.

3. In the **Before sheet** list box, select the worksheet before which the selected worksheet needs to be inserted.

4. Check the **Create a copy** check box if you want to copy the sheet, rather than move it, and click **OK.**

Procedure Reference: Rename a Worksheet Tab.

To rename a worksheet tab.

1. On the sheet tab bar, select the desired worksheet tab.

    - Right-click the worksheet tab and choose **Rename** or;

    - Double-click the worksheet tab.

2. Type the new name for the worksheet and press **Enter.**

Procedure Reference: Color Worksheet Tabs.

To color a worksheet tabs.

1. Select worksheet tab.

   ● Right-click the worksheet tab that you want to color, choose **Tab Color,** and select a color or;

   ● Select a worksheet tab, hold **Shift** and click another worksheet tab to select multiple worksheet tabs.

   ● Press **Ctrl** and click on the required worksheet tabs to select a non continuous range of worksheet tabs.

2. Color the worksheet tabs.

   ● Right-click the selected worksheet tabs that you want to color, choose **Tab Color,** and select a color or;

   ● On the **Home** tab, in the **Cells** group, from the **Format** drop-down list, select **Tab Color** and then select a color.

Procedure Reference: Hide or Unhide Worksheets

To hide or unhide worksheets:

1. Select the worksheets that you want to hide.

2. Right-click the selected tabs and choose **Hide** to hide the worksheets or in **Home** tab in the **Cells** group, from the **Format** drop-down list from the **Hide & Unhide** submenu select **Hide Sheet.**

3. If necessary, unhide the sheets.

   a. On the sheet tab bar, right-click any worksheet tab and choose **Unhide** or in **Home** tab in the **Cells** group, from the **Format** drop-down list from the **Hide & Unhide** submenu select **Unhide Sheet.**

   b. In the **Unhide** dialog box, in the **Unhide sheet** list box, select the hidden worksheet that you want to display and click **OK.**

ACTIVITY 5-1
Formatting Worksheet Tabs

Data Files:

C:\084576Data\Managing an Excel Workbook\Sales Summary.xlsx

Scenario:

The sales summary workbook comprises three worksheets, one for each region. Identifying the worksheet for the required region is difficult because the sheets are named with the default sheet names, instead of a descriptive label. You want to be able to readily recognize each region's worksheet.

---

1. Examine the three worksheets in the workbook.

   a. Navigate to the C:\084576Data\Managing an Excel Workbook folder and open the Sales Summary.xlsx file.

   b. Verify that the **Sheet1** tab contains data that is specific to the US division and select **Sheet2.**

   c. View the data that is specific to the Canadian division and select **Sheet3.**

   d. View the data that is specific to the Mexican division.

---

2. Rename the first worksheet.

   a. Select the **Sheet1** tab to display the US Sales Summary worksheet.

   b. On the sheet tab bar, right-click the **Sheet1** tab and choose **Rename.**

   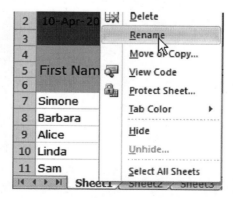

   c. Type *US* and press **Enter** to rename the tab.

---

3. Rename the second and third worksheets.

a. Double-click the **Sheet2** tab to rename Sheet2.

b. Type *Canada* and press **Enter.**

c. Similarly, rename the third worksheet as *Mexico*

---

4. Change the color of the worksheet tabs.

a. On the sheet tab bar, select the **US** tab.

b. On the **Home** tab, in the **Cells** group, from the **Format** drop-down list, select **Tab Color** and from the displayed gallery, in the **Standard Colors** section, select **Blue** which is the third color from right.

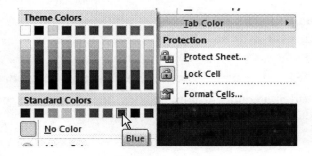

c. Select the **Canada** tab.

d. Right-click the **Canada** tab and move the mouse pointer over the **Tab Color** option.

e. From the displayed gallery, in the **Standard Colors** section, select **Yellow,** which is the fourth color from the left.

f. Similarly, change the color of the **Mexico** tab to green.

g. Save the workbook as *My Sales Summary* in XLSX format.

ACTIVITY 5-2
Organizing a Workbook

Before You Begin:

The My Sales Summary.xlsx file is open.

Scenario:

You have tracked the sales summary for each division in individual worksheets of an Excel workbook. You now need to add new worksheets to accommodate more data. Also, you want to organize and display these worksheets based on the sequence in which you want to access information. Moreover, you need to ensure that the worksheets meet the conditions mentioned below.

- The Mexico worksheet should appear before the Canada worksheet.
- A new sheet named Europe is needed for the new European division named Europe, which will have content similar to the Canada worksheet.
- Another new sheet is needed, which will contain the employee listing for all the divisions.
- Finally, the workbook is to be used at a couple of presentations, and at each presentation, you want only specific sheets to be displayed.

---

1. Move the Mexico worksheet to place it before the Canada worksheet.

    a. On the sheet tab bar, drag the **Mexico** tab to the left of the **Canada** tab.

    b. Observe that the **Mexico** tab appears before the **Canada** tab.

---

2. Copy the Canada worksheet.

a.	Right-click the **Canada** tab and choose **Move or Copy.**

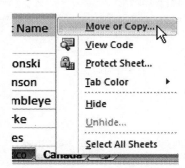

b.	In the **Move or Copy** dialog box, in the **To book** drop-down list, verify that the destination displayed is My Sales Summary.xlsx, and in the **Before sheet** list box, select **Canada.**

c.	Check the **Create a copy** check box and click **OK.**

d.	Observe that a copy of the worksheet, named Canada (2), is created.

3.	Modify the duplicated worksheet.

a.	Double-click the **Canada (2)** tab, type *Europe* and press **Enter** to rename the tab.

b.	Right-click the **Europe** tab, choose **Tab Color,** and in the **Standard Colors** section, select **Red.**

c.	Select cell **D2,** type *European Sales Summary* and press **Enter.**

d.	Select cell **A6,** hold down **Shift,** and click cell **I12.**

e.	On the **Home** tab, in the **Editing** group, click the **Clear** drop-down arrow and choose **Clear All.**

4.	Add a new worksheet to enter the employee listing for all the divisions.

a.	On the sheet tab bar, click the **Insert Worksheet** button to insert a new worksheet.

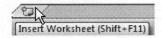

b.	Double-click the **Sheet2** tab, type *Employee Summary* and press **Enter.**

     c.   Apply the orange color to the **Employee Summary** tab.

5.   Hide all the worksheets, except the US worksheet.

     a.   Right-click the **Employee Summary** tab and choose **Hide.**

     b.   Select all the tabs from the **Mexico** tab to the **Canada** tab.

     c.   Right-click the selected tabs and choose **Hide.**

     d.   Observe that US is the only worksheet that is displayed and that the other worksheets are hidden.

 Data in the hidden worksheets is not deleted and the references to cells in the hidden worksheets are valid.

6.   Unhide the Canada and Mexico worksheets for use in another presentation.

     a.   Right-click the **US** tab and choose **Unhide.**

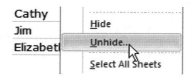

     b.   In the **Unhide sheet** list box, verify that **Mexico** is selected.

     c.   Click **OK** to display the worksheet.

     d.   Similarly, unhide the Canada worksheet.

     e.   Save the workbook.

TOPIC B
View Worksheets and Workbooks

You managed the worksheets in a workbook. You may want to view multiple worksheets of a workbook simultaneously or view different sections of a worksheet together. In this topic, you will view worksheets and workbooks.

When you are working on data that is spread over numerous pages, it is difficult to keep track of what information is on a particular page, or where new information is added. You may also need to check the column or row headings multiple times to know whether you are looking at the correct cell. Excel provides you with various views to work with worksheets and to ensure that the column and row headings are always visible.

Freeze Panes Options

By freezing panes, you can keep a particular portion of a worksheet static, while you scroll through the other areas. You can access the **Freeze Panes** options from the **Freeze Panes** drop-down list in the **Window** group on the **View** tab. When you select the **Freeze Panes** option, the option toggles to display the **Unfreeze Panes** option that allows you to unfreeze panes. Excel allows you to freeze the top row, first column, or panes in a worksheet.

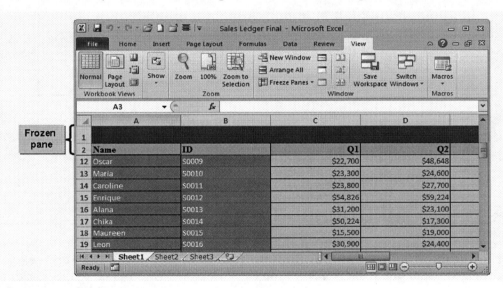

Figure 5-4: *A freezed header row in a worksheet.*

Option	Allows You To
Freeze Panes	Keep the portion of the worksheet above the selected row and to the left of the selected column static, while you scroll through the other rows and columns.
Freeze Top Row	Keep the top row static, while you scroll through the other rows of the worksheet.
Freeze First Column	Keep the first column static, while you scroll through the other columns of the worksheet.

Option	Allows You To
Unfreeze Panes	Unfreeze panes and enable you to scroll through the entire worksheet.

The Split Command

When you work with large worksheets, you may need to view different portions of a worksheet simultaneously. Using the **Split** command, you can split the worksheet into multiple resizable panes to view its various parts by scrolling through different panes. You can resize these panes by dragging the split bars that separate them.

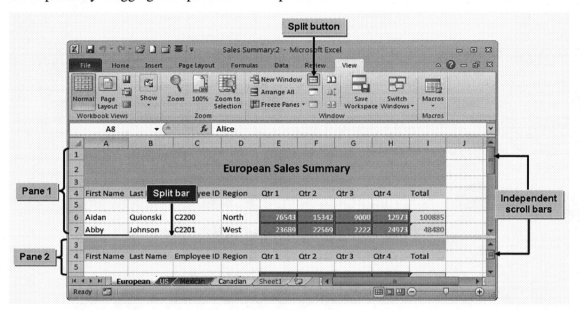

Figure 5-5: A window displaying split panes of a worksheet.

The Arrange All Command

The **Arrange All** command enables you to arrange all open windows side by side on the screen. The **Arrange Windows** dialog box contains options to specify how the workbook windows are arranged within the Excel window. You can check the **Windows of active workbook** check box to display only the windows of the current workbook. Excel provides you with options to arrange windows in a tiled, horizontal, vertical, or cascade arrangement.

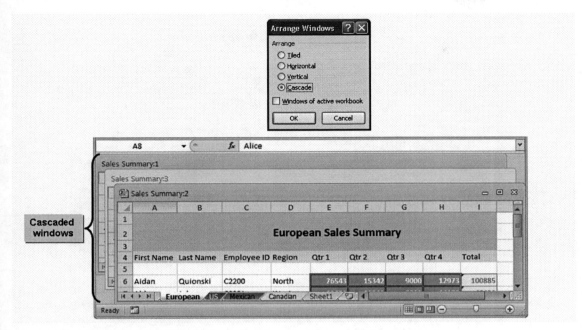

Figure 5-6: *The Arrange Windows dialog box and cascaded worksheets.*

Option	Used To
Tiled	View all the open windows as rectangles, covering the entire Excel window.
Horizontal	View all the open windows, one below the other.
Vertical	View all the open windows, one next to the other.
Cascade	View all the open windows, displayed one behind the other.

The View Side by Side Command

You can view and compare two different Excel workbooks or different parts of the same worksheet simultaneously by using the **View Side by Side** command. When you tile two workbook windows using this command, both windows scroll simultaneously because the **Synchronous Scrolling** command is enabled by default. You can disable synchronous scrolling by clicking the **Synchronous Scrolling** button. You can use the **Reset Window Position** command to reset a workbook window to its original position.

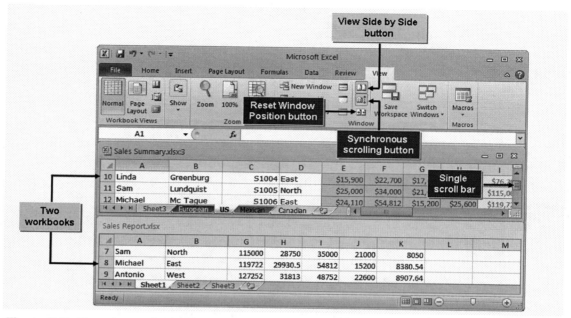

Figure 5-7: *Two views of a workbooks arranged side by side.*

The Switch Windows Command

The **Switch Windows** command allows you to switch views between the workbook windows that are open. You can switch to and view different workbooks that are open without maximizing or minimizing each workbook window. When you click the **Switch Windows** drop-down arrow, a list of open workbooks is displayed. You can select the desired workbook from this list to display it.

The New Window Command

The **New Window** command allows you to view the same worksheet in another workbook window. This will enable you to use the **View Side by Side** command to compare and edit different sections of the same worksheet.

How to View Worksheets and Workbooks

Procedure Reference: Freeze or Unfreeze Panes

To freeze or unfreeze panes:

1. Select the worksheet in which you want to freeze or unfreeze panes.

2. Freeze the panes.

    ●   On the **View** tab, in the **Window** group, click the **Freeze Panes** drop-down arrow and select **Freeze Top Row** or **Freeze First Column** to freeze only the first row or column.

    ●   Select the cell that is below the row and to the right of the column that you want to freeze, and on the **View** tab, in the **Window** group, click the **Freeze Panes** drop-down arrow and select **Freeze Panes** to freeze both rows and columns.

3. If necessary, on the **View** tab, in the **Window** group, click the **Freeze Panes** drop-down arrow and select **Unfreeze Panes** to unfreeze the panes.

Procedure Reference: Split a Worksheet Window

To split a worksheet window:

1. Select the cell in a worksheet where you want to split the worksheet window.

2. On the Ribbon, on the **View** tab, in the **Window** group, click **Split.**

3. If necessary, click the **Split** button again to undo the split action.

Procedure Reference: Arrange the Worksheets in Separate Windows Within an Excel Window

To arrange the worksheets in separate windows within a workbook:

1. With a workbook open, on the **View** tab, in the **Window** group, click **New Window** to open the entire workbook in a new window.

2. Repeat step 1 until you have a new window for every worksheet that you want to view in a new window.

3. In the **Window** group, click **Arrange All** to display the **Arrange Windows** dialog box and select the desired display option.

4. If you have multiple workbooks open, check the **Windows of active workbook** check box to avoid arranging the windows of other open workbooks and click **OK.**

Procedure Reference: View Different Sections of a Worksheet Side by Side

To view different sections of a worksheet side by side:

1. With a workbook open, on the **View** tab, in the **Window** group, click **New Window** to open the entire workbook in another window.

2. In the Window group, click the **View Side by Side** button.

3. If necessary, click the **View Side by Side** button again to undo the action.

ACTIVITY 5-3
Viewing a Large Worksheet

Data Files:

C:\084576Data\Managing an Excel Workbook\Sales Ledger Final.xlsx

Before You Begin:

The My Sales Summary.xlsx file is open.

Scenario:

You are reviewing the data in the sales report. Due to the large amount of data in the sheet, you find it difficult to identify and focus on specific data. You also want to compare the sales values in the US division, Canadian division, and Mexican division worksheets. You need to be able to view the content simultaneously in all the three worksheets.

---

1. Split the US worksheet window.

   a. Select the **US** tab.

   b. Scroll through the worksheet that is displayed to view its data.

   c. Observe that once you scroll down to see the information in row 31, the column headings are no longer visible.

   d. Scroll up and select cell **E16**.

   e. Select the **View** tab, and in the **Window** group, click **Split** to display the vertical and horizontal split bars.

   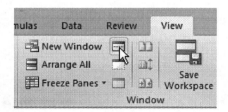

   f. In the top-right pane, click the scroll bar to scroll down the top pane.

   g. Observe that the pane below is stationary, while both the panes at the top scroll simultaneously.

   h. At the bottom-right corner, click the scroll bar and scroll down the pane to compare different segments of the worksheet.

   i. On the **View** tab, in the **Window** group, click the **Split** button again to undo the split action.

---

2. Freeze panes and view data.

   a. If necessary, scroll up and select cell **A7**.

---

b. On the **View** tab, in the **Window** group, from the **Freeze Panes** drop-down list, select **Freeze Panes.**

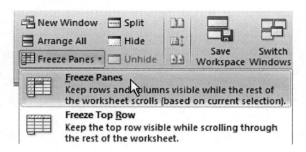

c. In the worksheet, scroll down to row 33.

d. Observe that the column headings are visible, while the rest of the worksheet can be scrolled through.

e. In the **Window** group, from the **Freeze Panes** drop-down list, select **Unfreeze Panes.**

3. Create two new windows to view two copies of a worksheet.

a. In the **Window** group, click **New Window.**

b. Observe that the My Sales Summary workbook opens in a new window with the title My Sales Summary.xlsx:2 - Microsoft Excel.

c. In the **Window** group, click **New Window** to create a another new window with the title My Sales Summary.xlsx:3 - Microsoft Excel.

d. Select cell **A7** and press **Delete** to delete the data in the cell.

e. On the **View** tab, in the **Window** group, click the **Switch Window** drop-down arrow.

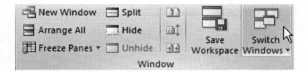

f. From the **Switch Window** drop-down list, select **My Sales Summary:.xlsx.2** and observe that the same content is deleted in this workbook.

g. On the Quick Access toolbar, click the **Undo** button to undo the delete action.

4. View the windows arranged in different styles.

a. In the **Window** group, click **Arrange All** to display the **Arrange Windows** dialog box.

b.   In the **Arrange Windows** dialog box, select the **Vertical** option and click **OK.**

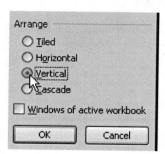

c.   Observe that the three workbook windows are displayed vertically one beside the other.

d.   On the **View** tab, in the **Window** group, click the **Arrange All** button, and in the **Arrange Windows** dialog box, select the **Cascade** option and click **OK.**

e.   Observe that the windows now appear cascaded one behind the other and close the My Sales Summary.xlsx:3 - Microsoft Excel and My Sales Summary.xlsx:2 - Microsoft Excel windows.

5.   View the windows side by side.

a.   On the Quick Access toolbar, click the **Open** button.

b.   From the C:\084576Data\Managing an Excel Workbook folder, open the Sales Ledger Final.xlsx file.

c.   On the **View** tab, in the **Window** group, click the **View Side by Side** button.

d.   Observe that the windows are displayed one after another and then click on the scroll bar to scroll down the worksheet and close the Sales Ledger Final.xlsx file.

e.   Save and close the My Sales Summary.xlsx file.

Lesson 5 Follow-up

In this lesson, you managed an Excel workbook. This skill will enable you to efficiently access and view specific areas of a worksheet.

1. **How do you think Excel's tools to manage multiple worksheets will be useful to you?**

2. **In what ways can you customize the display of worksheets in Excel?**

6 | Printing Excel Workbooks

Lesson Time: 45 minutes

Lesson Objectives:

In this lesson, you will print the content of an Excel worksheet.

You will:

- Define the page layout.
- Print a workbook.

Introduction

You worked with a large workbook. You may now want to share a worksheet with others. One way to share the content of a worksheet is by printing it. In this lesson, you will print the content of an Excel workbook.

You may be faced with situations where you want to share the content of a worksheet and need a printout of it. Excel provides you with various options to print a workbook. The **Print** option in Excel is integrated with the Backstage view, and provides you with the ability to print worksheets with just a few mouse clicks.

TOPIC A
Define the Page Layout

You used various methods to manage a workbook. The workbook is finalized and now ready to be printed. Before printing, you want to adjust the print options that help you customize the output to meet your needs. In this topic, you will define the page layout for a worksheet.

Before printing a workbook, you need to check and adjust the page layout so that the printed output looks professional. To achieve the desired print output, you may need to adjust the layout of the worksheets, add headers and footers, or change the page orientation. Excel provides you with various page layout options for customizing workbooks and improving their appearance on the printed material.

Headers and Footers

Definition:

A *header* or *footer* is a data block that comprises text and graphics displayed at the top or bottom of a printed page. By default, Excel headers and footers contain three placeholders at the left, center, and right edges of a page, respectively. You can include information in any of the three placeholders in a header or footer. Each placeholder can contain text or graphics that will remain the same for all pages, or text that changes based on some criteria, such as the page number.

Example:

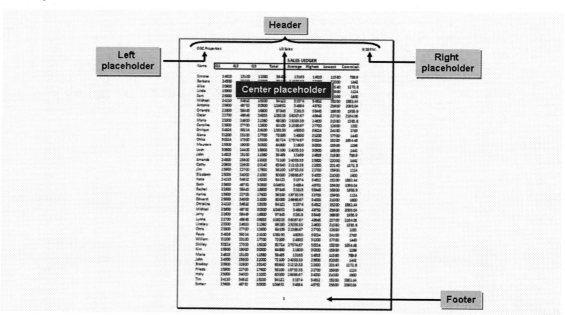

Figure 6-1: *A worksheet with a header and footer.*

Header and Footer Settings

Excel provides you with options to either use predefined or create custom headers and footers. Headers and footers are displayed only in the **Page Layout** view and on printed pages. Predefined settings allow you to insert page numbers, page count, sheet numbers, predefined text, and current date in a predefined layout. Alternatively, you can create custom headers and footers that enable you to enter content in the left, center, and right header or footer text box. You can also define different headers and footers for odd and even pages if you want a worksheet to be printed in a book style. In addition, you can remove the header and footer from the first printed page that usually displays the title.

Figure 6-2: Header and footer settings displayed on the Design contextual tab.

Page Margins

A *page margin* is a boundary line that determines the amount of space between the worksheet data and the edge of the paper. Page margins define a region within which the content of a page should fit in. Excel provides you with options to select from a list of predefined margins or specify a custom value for page margins. You can set the top, bottom, left, and right margins. You can also adjust the distance of the header from the top of the page and the distance of the footer from the bottom of the page. You can set the option to print the data at the center of the page horizontally and vertically.

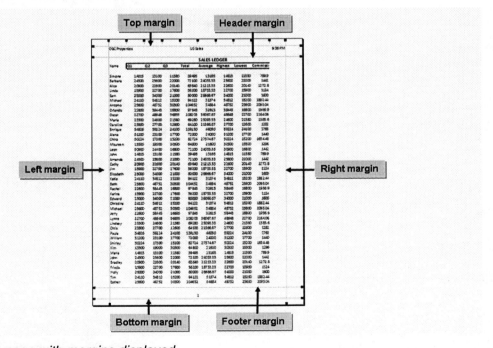

Figure 6-3: A page with margins displayed.

Margins Tab Options

The options on the **Margins** tab allow you to set margin sizes for either an entire worksheet or only the current section.

Option	Enables You To
The **Left, Top, Header, Right, Bottom,** and **Footer** spin boxes	Set the respective margin values by using the up or down arrow or by entering a value for the margin.
The **Center on page** section	Specify whether the content should be centered horizontally or vertically on a printed page.
The **Print** button	Set the print options in the Backstage view.
The **Print Preview** button	Preview a worksheet.
The **Options** button	Set the document properties for the print output.

Page Orientation

Page orientation is a page layout setting that determines the layout of the content on a printed page. It specifies whether a page is to be printed vertically or horizontally. In the **Portrait** orientation, the height of the page will be greater than the width; this enables you to print more rows of data, but fewer columns. In the **Landscape** orientation, the width will be greater than the height; this enables you to print more columns of data, but fewer rows.

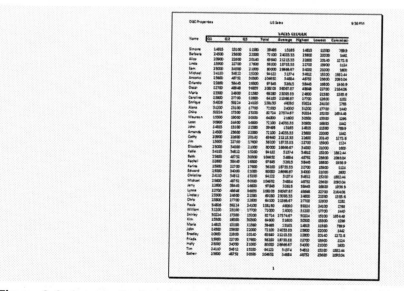

Figure 6-4: *A page displayed in the Portrait layout.*

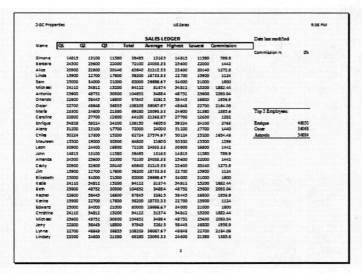

Figure 6-5: *A page displayed in the Landscape layout.*

The Print Titles Command

When a worksheet containing data that runs across multiple pages is printed, you can use the **Print Titles** command to repeat the row and column titles on each printed page of a worksheet. Repeating the row and column titles enables you to identify and interpret the content in a worksheet easily. You can set print titles by using the **Print Titles** section on the **Sheet** tab in the **Page Setup** dialog box.

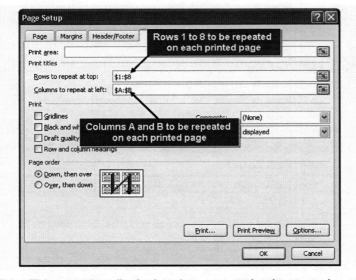

Figure 6-6: *The Print Titles section displaying the rows and columns to be repeated.*

Print Row and Column Headings

The **Page Setup** dialog box provides you with an option to print the numerical row headings that are at the left of the worksheet rows and the alphabetical column headings that appear at the top of the columns on a worksheet.

Page Breaks

Definition:

Page breaks are lines that split content across pages for print purposes. They are determined based on the paper size, page orientation, and any existing page breaks. Page breaks generated by the application are referred to as automatic page breaks, and those that are manually inserted are referred to as manual page breaks. You can convert an automatic page break to a manual page break by repositioning it at a preferred location.

Example:

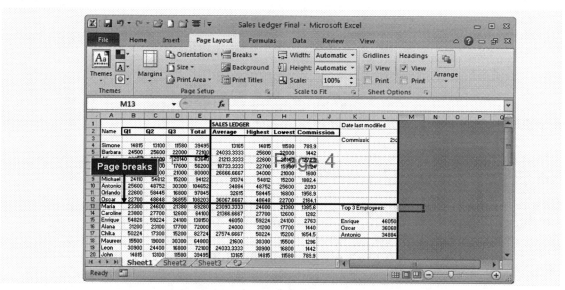

Figure 6-7: *Page breaks marking where the content will be split when printing.*

Page Break Options

You can insert or remove manual page breaks in a worksheet by using the options available in Excel.

Option	Allows You To
Insert Page Break	Insert a manual page break either above or to the left of a selected row or column.
Remove Page Break	Remove an existing manual page break from either above or the left of a selected row or column.
Reset All Page Breaks	Remove all the manual page breaks from a worksheet.

Gridlines

Gridlines are thin lines that divide a worksheet into rows and columns. Printing gridlines enables you to read and reference information presented on a printed worksheet easily. You can also change the color of the gridlines based on your preference.

How to Define the Page Layout

Procedure Reference: Insert a Header and Footer in an Excel Spreadsheet

To insert a header and footer in an Excel spreadsheet:

1. Open an Excel workbook.

2. Select the spreadsheet to which you want to add the header and footer.

3. Select the **Page Layout** view.

    -   On the **View** tab, in the **Workbook Views** group, click **Page Layout** or;

    -   On the **Insert** tab, in the **Text** group, click **Header & Footer** or;

    -   On the status bar, next to the **Zoom Level** button, click the **Page Layout** button.

4. Insert the header and footer.

    -   On the **Header & Footer Tools** tool tab, on the **Design** contextual tab, in the **Header & Footer** group, click **Header** or **Footer,** and from the displayed list, select an option to insert a predefined header and footer or;

    -   On the header or footer, click the left, center, or right text box and enter the desired text to create a custom header and footer.

5. Click any cell outside the text boxes to deselect the header or footer text box.

6. If necessary, return to the **Normal** view.

    -   On the **View** tab, in the **Workbook Views** group, click **Normal** or;

    -   On the status bar, next to the **Zoom** slider, click the **Normal** button.

7. If necessary, in the **Page Setup** dialog box, on the **Header/Footer** tab, specify the desired header and footer option.

    -   Check the **Different odd and even pages** check box to specify that the headers and footers on the odd-numbered pages should be different from those on the even-numbered pages.

    -   Check the **Different First Page** check box to remove headers and footers from the first printed page.

Procedure Reference: Create or Modify a Header or Footer by Using the Page Setup Dialog Box

To create or modify a header or footer by using the **Page Setup** dialog box:

1. Display the **Page Setup** dialog box and select the **Header/Footer** tab.

2. From the **Header** or **Footer** drop-down list, select a predefined header or footer.

3. If necessary, click **Custom Header** or **Custom Footer** and enter data in the left, center, or right header text box.

4. Click **OK** to apply the header or footer settings.

Procedure Reference: Set the Page Margins

To set the page margins:

1. On the **Page Layout** tab, in the **Page Setup** group, click **Margins,** and from the displayed list, select the desired option.

    *   Select **Normal** to set top and bottom margins of 0.75 inches and left and right margins of 0.7 inches.

    *   Select **Wide** to set 1 inch top, bottom, left, and right margins and 0.5 inches separating the header and footer from the top and bottom margins.

    *   Select **Narrow** to set top and bottom margins of 0.75 inches, left and right margins of 0.25 inches with 0.3 inches separating the header and footer from the top and bottom margins.

2. Select **Custom Margins,** and in the displayed dialog box, specify the desired option to customize the margins.

 You can also set the page margins in the Backstage view. In the preview pane, click the **Show Margins** button to display the margin guides that you can use to reposition the margins.

Procedure Reference: Change the Page Orientation

To change the page orientation:

1. Change the orientation of a worksheet.

    *   In the **Page Setup** dialog box, on the **Page** tab, in the **Orientation** section, select an option.

        *   Select **Portrait** to print the worksheet vertically.

        *   Select **Landscape** to print the worksheet horizontally.

    *   On the **Page Layout** tab, in the **Page Setup** group, click **Orientation** and select an option.

    *   On the **File** tab, select **Print,** and in the **Print** pane, from the **Portrait Orientation** drop-down list, select an option.

2. Save the worksheet with the new orientation.

Procedure Reference: Set or Remove a Print Title

To set or remove a print title:

1. On the **Page Layout** tab, in the **Page Setup** group, click **Print Titles.**

2. In the **Page Setup** dialog box, on the **Sheet** tab, specify a print title or remove an existing print title.

    *   In the **Print Titles** section, click the **Rows to repeat at top** or **Columns to repeat at left** text box and select the rows or columns that need to be used as the print title.

 You can click the **Collapse Dialog** button to the right of the **Print Title** text box to minimize the **Page Setup** dialog box and make it easier to select data in a worksheet. Press **Enter** or click the **Expand Dialog** button to maximize the dialog box when you are done. Clicking anywhere in a row or column will select the entire row or column.

- In the **Rows to repeat at top** and **Columns to repeat at left** text boxes, delete any text that is already set and click **OK** to remove an existing print title.

3. In the **Page Setup** dialog box, click **OK** to apply the changes.

Procedure Reference: Insert Page Breaks

To insert page breaks:

1. Select the row below or the column to the right of the location where you want to insert a page break.

2. Insert a page break.

- On the **Page Layout** tab, in the **Page Setup** group, click **Breaks,** and from the displayed list, select **Insert Page Break** or;

- Insert page breaks using **Page Break Preview.**

  a. Enable **Page Break Preview.**

     - Click the **Page Break Preview** button or;

     - On the **View** tab, in the **Workbook Views** group, click **Page Break Preview.**

  b. Set the page breaks.

     - In the Page Break Preview window, drag the automatic page break to the desired position or;

     - On the worksheet, right-click a cell adjacent to the page break and choose **Insert Page Break** or;

     - In the worksheet, select the desired row or column, right-click the selected row or column, and choose **Insert Page Break.**

  c. Return to the **Normal** view.

 The benefit of the Page Break Preview window is that it shows the order in which the pages will be printed in addition to where the page breaks will occur.

Procedure Reference: Remove Page Breaks

To remove page breaks:

1. Select the row below or the column to the right of a manual page break that you want to remove.

2. Remove the page break.

- On the **Page Layout** tab, in the **Page Setup** group, click **Breaks,** and from the displayed list, select **Remove Page Break** or;

 You can reset all the existing manual page breaks in a worksheet by using the **Reset All Page Break** option in the drop-down list.

- Remove page breaks using **Page Break Preview.**

  a. Enable **Page Break Preview.**

- Click the **Page Break Preview** button or;
- On the **View** tab, in the **Workbook Views** group, click **Page Break Preview.**

b. Remove the page breaks.

- In the Page Break Preview window, drag the automatic page break off the worksheet.
- In the worksheet, select the desired row or column, right-click the selected row or column, and choose **Remove Page Break.**

c. Return to the **Normal** view.

ACTIVITY 6-1
Adding Headers and Footers

Data Files:

C:\084576Data\Printing Excel Workbooks\Sales Ledger Final.xlsx

Scenario:

You will be presenting a report on the sales revenue of your team. You want to distribute the printed copies of the sales report to other managers. You decide to add the header and footer information to the printed copies and preview the worksheet.

---

1. Create the header.

    a. Navigate to the C:\084576Data\Printing Excel Workbooks folder, open the Sales Ledger Final.xlsx file and maximize the file.

    b. Select the **Insert** tab, and in the **Text** group, click **Header & Footer.**

     Excel displays the worksheet in the **Page Layout** view.

    c. In the left header text box, click and type *OGC Stores*

    d. In the center header text box, click and type *US Sales*

    e. Click the right header text box, and in the **Header and Footer Tools** tool tab, on the **Design** contextual tab, in the **Header & Footer Elements** group, click **Current Time.**

---

2. Create the footer.

    a. On the **Header & Footer Tools** tool tab, on the **Design** contextual tab, in the **Navigation** group, click **Go to Footer.**

    b. Click the center footer text box, and on the **Design** contextual tab, in the **Header & Footer** group, click the **Footer** drop-down arrow, and from the displayed list, select **Page 1 of ?.**

---

3. Preview the header and footer information.

    a. On the **File** tab, choose **Print.**

    b. In the right pane, observe the preview of the worksheet.

---

c. In the Backstage view, at the bottom-right corner of the right pane, click the **Zoom to Page** button, to increase the magnification and view the header information.

d. Observe that the text "OGC Stores" and "US Sales" are included in the header and scroll to the right.

e. Observe that the current time is included in the right section of the header and that the page orientation does not accommodate the other column and scroll down.

f. Observe that the footer information displays the page number.

g. Click the **Zoom to Page** button to decrease the magnification level.

h. Save the worksheet as *My Sales Ledger Final*

ACTIVITY 6-2
Setting the Page Layout and Previewing a Worksheet

Before you Begin:
The My Sales Ledger Final.xlsx file is open.

Scenario:
While previewing the sales report worksheet, you notice that the page orientation does not accommodate all the columns in one page. You also want the Name and ID columns to be displayed on all the printed pages. You observe that the worksheet is not split logically with some of the data on one page and the rest of the data on the next page. You decide to modify the page breaks to print the worksheet correctly.

---

1. Set the page orientation to **Landscape.**

    a. Select the **View** tab, and in the **Workbook Views** group, click **Page Break Preview.**

    b. In the **Welcome to Page Break Preview** dialog box, click **OK.**

    c. Scroll up to view the worksheet.

    d. Select the **Page Layout** tab, and in the **Page Setup** group, click **Orientation,** and from the displayed list, select **Landscape.**

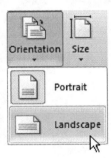

---

2. Preview the worksheet.

    a.   Select the **File** tab and choose **Print.**

    b.   In the right pane, observe that the page is displayed horizontally, the Name and ID columns are displayed, and the columns are displayed only till the Lowest column.

    c.   In the right pane, click the **Next Page** button.

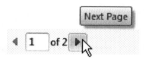

    d.   Observe that the second page displays data which does not correspond to the data on the previous page.

---

3. Insert a manual page break between columns G and H.

    a.   Select the **File** tab to close the Backstage view.

    b.   In the worksheet, click the page break between the columns I and J and drag it between the columns G and H.

    c.   Select the **File** tab and choose **Print.**

    d.   Observe that the first page contains information up to the average column and then click the **Next Page** button.

    e.   Observe that the name columns are not displayed on page 2, making it difficult to know which row corresponds to which employee.

---

4. Set the First Name and ID as print titles.

    a.   Select the **File** tab to close the Backstage view.

    b.   On the **Page Layout** tab, in the **Page Setup** group, click **Print Titles.**

    c.   In the **Page Setup** dialog box, on the **Sheet** tab, in the **Print Titles** section, in the **Columns to repeat at left** text box, click and type *A:B* d.　Click **OK** to close the **Page Setup** dialog box.

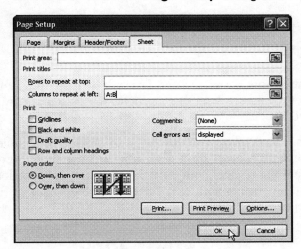

5.　Preview the entire Sales Ledger worksheet.

a.　Select the **File** tab and choose **Print.**

b.　Observe that the preview of the first page of the worksheet is displayed in the right pane of the Backstage view.

c.　Click the **Next Page** button.

d.　Observe that the second page of the worksheet displays the print titles.

e.　Save the worksheet.

TOPIC B
Print a Workbook

You set the page layout options to control how the worksheet data will be displayed in print. You are now ready to print a worksheet to share it with other people. In this topic, you will specify the print options and print a workbook.

You have presented key information in a worksheet. You now want to make it accessible to those who do not have access to a computer. Moreover, in a worksheet containing a large amount of data, you may want to present the readers with only the necessary information. By printing selective data, you can present the readers with only the relevant information. Excel provides you with various options to print a worksheet.

The Print Options in the Backstage View

The **Print** command allows you to preview and print a worksheet. The print options are displayed in the Backstage view. The left pane of the Backstage view consists of the options to print a document, specify the printer, and set the printer settings. The right pane displays the preview of a worksheet and includes options to scroll through pages and display page margins. The right pane also provides you with the option to zoom in or zoom out of a previewed page.

Print Section	*Enables You To*
Print	Set the number of copies that need to be printed and print a worksheet.
Printer	Select a printer from a list of available printers. It also allows you to set the printer properties.
Settings	Select the range of pages, specify the page orientation, select a paper size, and set the margins.

Printing Selected Worksheets

The **Settings** section allows you to print selected worksheets by first selecting the worksheets that you want to print and then selecting the **Print Active Sheets** option from the **Settings** drop-down list in the Backstage view.

Printing an Entire Workbook

The **Settings** section allows you to print an entire workbook by first selecting any of the worksheets and then selecting the **Print Entire Workbook** option from the **Settings** drop-down list in the Backstage view.

The Print Area

The *print area* is a particular portion of a worksheet that you need to print often by selecting the desired area in the worksheet. By default, when you print a worksheet, Excel prints the defined print area. The options in the **Print Area** drop-down list allow you to set or clear the print area. You can also add another selection to the print area by using the **Add to Print Area** option.

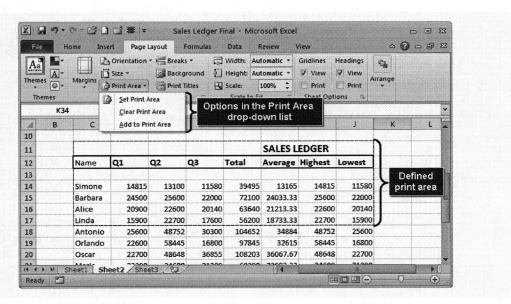

Figure 6-8: A marquee displaying the print area.

Scaling Options

The scaling options in the **Scale to Fit** group on the **Page Layout** tab enable you to restrict the printed output of a worksheet to a desired number of pages. You can scale to shrink or increase the width or height of a worksheet to fit within a desired number of pages, or you can shrink or increase the worksheet to a specific percentage of the actual size. You can also use the **Adjust to** and **Fit to** options on the **Page** tab in the **Page Setup** dialog box to set the scaling for a worksheet.

Figure 6-9: Various scaling options in the Scale to Fit group.

How to Print a Workbook

Procedure Reference: Set or Clear the Print Area

To set or clear the print area:

1. In a worksheet, select the cells that you want to set as the print area, or select the cells that are currently set as the print area.

2. On the **Page Layout** tab, in the **Page Setup** group, click **Print Area** and select **Set Print Area** or **Clear Print Area.**

3. If necessary, select specific cells, and from the **Print Area** drop-down list, select **Add to Print Area** to add additional ranges of cells to the print area.

4. Save the worksheet with the new print area settings.

Procedure Reference: Scale the Printable Range

To scale the printable range:

1. Scale the printable range.

   - On the **Page Layout** tab, in the **Scale to Fit** group, select the **Height, Width,** or **Scale** option to scale the range or;

   - Open the **Page Setup** dialog box, and on the **Page** tab, in the **Scaling** section, scale the range to adjust the scaling to a specific percentage, or fit the whole spreadsheet within a specified number of pages.

2. If necessary, preview and print the workbook.

3. Save the workbook with the scaled settings.

Procedure Reference: Print an Excel Worksheet

To print an Excel worksheet:

1. Select the **File** tab and choose **Print.**

2. In the Backstage view, in the left pane, in the **Print** section, in the **Copies** spin box, specify the number of copies that you need.

3. In the **Printer** section, from the **Printer** drop-down list, select a printer.

4. If necessary, click the **Printer Properties** link to set the properties of the printer.

5. In the **Settings** section, in the **Pages** and **to** spin boxes, specify the page range.

6. From the **Collation** drop-down list, select **Collated** to completely print the first set of the selected pages and then the next set of copies when you are printing multiple copies.

7. In the right pane, preview the worksheet and click **Print.**

ACTIVITY 6-3
Setting the Print Area

Before You Begin:
The My Sales Ledger Final.xlsx file is open.

Scenario:
You need to present the entire report to your manager periodically in a single page format. You decide to define a print area and set the options to scale the content to be printed.

---

1. Preview the range of cells that needs to be printed.

   a. Select the **View** tab, and in the **WorkBook Views** group, click the **Normal** button to view the workbook in the normal view.

   b. Select the cell range **A1:J20.**

    If you forget to select the range, or forget to select **Selection** in the **Print** dialog box, the entire worksheet will be displayed in the preview.

   c. Select the **File** tab and choose **Print.**

   d. In the Backstage view, in the **Settings** section, from the **Print Active Sheets** drop-down list, select **Print Selection.**

   e. Observe that the selected range is displayed in two pages in the right pane of the Backstage view.

   f. Select the **File** tab to return to the worksheet.

---

2. Set the selected range of cells as the print area.

   a. Verify that the cell range A1:J20 is selected. Select the **Page Layout** tab, and in the **Page Setup** group, click **Print Area** and select **Set Print Area.**

   b. Click any cell to deselect the selected range.

   c. Observe the marquee around the cell range A1:J20 that indicates the set print area.

   d. Select the **File** tab and choose **Print.**

   e. In the Backstage view, in the **Settings** section, from the **Print Selection** drop-down list, select **Print Active Sheets.**

---

    f.   Observe that the print area that is set is displayed in two pages in the print preview.

    g.   Select the **File** tab to close the Backstage view.

3.   Change the color of the gridlines.

    a.   On the **Page Layout** tab, in the **Sheet Options** group, in the **Gridlines** section, check the **Print** check box.

    b.   Select the **File** tab and choose **Options.**

    c.   In the **Excel Options** dialog box, select the **Advanced** tab, scroll down, and in the **Display options for this worksheet** section, click the **Gridline color** drop-down arrow and select **Dark Red,** which is the first color in the second row.

    d.   Click **OK** to close the **Excel Options** dialog box.

    e.   Observe that the gridlines in the worksheet are displayed in red.

4.   Scale and print the data in the entire worksheet.

    a.   On the **Page Layout** tab, in the **Scale to Fit** group, from the **Width** drop-down list, select **1 page** to fit the width of the data in the worksheet within a single page.

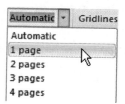

    b.   Select the **File** tab and choose **Print.**

    c.   Observe that the print area of the worksheet fits within a single page.

    d.   In the **Print** section, click **Print** to print the worksheet with the new settings.

    e.   Save the worksheet and close it.

    f.   Close the application.

Lesson 6 Follow-up

In this lesson, you printed a worksheet. Printing selective data saves paper when only small subsets of a worksheet are to be printed and it also helps readers view only the data that is necessary to them.

1. **Which page layout option will you use frequently? Why?**

2. **How do you think the Print Area option will be beneficial to you?**

Follow-up

In this course, you used Excel to manage, edit, and print data. Storing data electronically is more efficient than storing it in a paper-based system because it allows you to quickly update existing data, run reports on the data, calculate totals, and sort and filter data.

1. **Consider your current work environment. What are the advantages if the entire project is controlled and manipulated within Excel?**

2. **What specific techniques in this course did you find the most interesting and useful?**

3. **How does the Backstage view help you in printing workbooks?**

What's Next?

Microsoft® Office Excel® 2010: Level 2 is the next course in this series.

A Microsoft Office Excel 2010 Exam 77–882

Selected Element K courseware addresses Microsoft Office Specialist certification skills for Microsoft Office 2010. The following table indicates where Excel 2010 skills are covered. For example, 3-A indicates the lesson and topic number applicable to that skill, and 3-1 indicates the lesson and activity number.

Objective Domain	Level	Topic	Activity
1. Managing the Worksheet Environment			
1.1 Navigate through a worksheet			
1.1.1 Use hot keys	1	1-B	1-2
1.1.2 Use the name box	1	1-A, 3-B	1-2, 3-2
1.2 Print a worksheet or workbook			
1.2.1 Print only selected worksheets	1	6-B	
1.2.2 Print an entire workbook	1	6-B	
1.2.3 Construct headers and footers	1	6-A	6-1
1.2.4 Apply printing options			
1.2.4.1 Scale	1	6-B	6-3
1.2.4.2 Print titles	1	6-A	6-2
1.2.4.3 Page setup	1	6-A	6-2, 6-3
1.2.4.4 Print area	1	6-B	6-3
1.2.4.5 Gridlines	1	6-A	6-3
1.3 Personalize the environment by using Backstage			
1.3.1 Manipulate the Quick Access Toolbar	1	1-A, 1-C	1–1, 1–3
1.3.2 Customize the ribbon	2	6-A	6-1
1.3.2.1 Tabs	1	1-C	
1.3.2.2 Groups	1	1-C	
1.3.3 Manipulate Excel default settings (Excel Options)	1	1-C	1-3
1.3.4 Manipulate workbook properties (document panel)	3	1-A	
1.3.5 Manipulate workbook files and folders			

Objective Domain	Level	Topic	Activity
1.3.5.1 Manage versions	2	6-A	
1.3.5.2 AutoSave	2	6-A	
2. Creating Cell Data			
2.1 Construct cell data			
2.1.1 Use paste special			
2.1.1.1 Formats	1	4-D	
2.1.1.2 Formulas	1	4-D	
2.1.1.3 Values	1	4-D	
2.1.1.4 Preview icons	2	6-A	
2.1.1.5 Transpose rows	1	3-A	3-1
2.1.1.6 Transpose columns	1	3-A	
2.1.1.7 Operations			
2.1.1.7.1 Add	1	4-D	
2.1.1.7.2 Divide	1	4-D	
2.1.1.8 Comments	1	4-D	
2.1.1.9 Validation	1	4-D	
2.1.1.10 Paste as a link	1	4-D	
2.1.2 Cut	1	2-C	
2.1.3 Move	1	2-C	3-1
2.1.4 Select cell data	1	1-B	1-2
2.2 Apply AutoFill			
2.2.1 Copy data	1	3-A	
2.2.2 Fill a series	1	3-A	3-1
2.2.3 Preserve cell format	1	3-A	
2.3 Apply and manipulate hyperlinks			
2.3.1 Create a hyperlink in a cell	2	6-B	6-2
2.3.2 Modify hyperlinks	2	6-B	
2.3.3 Modify hyperlinked cell attributes	2	6-B	
2.3.4 Remove a hyperlink	2	6-B	
3. Formatting Cells and Worksheets			
3.1 Apply and modify cell formats			
3.1.1 Align cell content	1	4-C	4-3
3.1.2 Apply a number format	1	4-D	4-4
3.1.3 Wrapping text in a cell	1	4-C	4-3
3.1.4 Use Format Painter	1	4-A	4-2
3.2 Merge or split cells			
3.2.1 Use Merge & Center	1	4-C	4-3
3.2.2 Merge Across	1	4-C	
3.2.3 Merge cells	1	4-C	
3.2.4 Unmerge Cells	1	4-C	

Objective Domain	Level	Topic	Activity
3.3 Create row and column titles			
3.3.1 Print row and column headings	1	6-A	
3.3.2 Print rows to repeat with titles	1	6-A	6-2
3.3.3 Print columns to repeat with titles	1	6-A	
3.3.4 Configure titles to print only on odd or even pages	1	6-A	
3.3.5 Configure titles to skip the first worksheet page	1	6-A	
3.4 Hide or unhide rows and columns			
3.4.1 Hide or unhide a column	1	3-C	
3.4.2 Hide or unhide a row	1	3-C	
3.4.3 Hide a series of columns	1	3-C	3-4
3.4.4 Hide a series of rows	1	3-C	
3.5 Manipulate Page Setup options for worksheets			
3.5.1 Configure page orientation	1	6-A	6-2
3.5.2 Manage page scaling	1	6-B	
3.5.3 Configure page margins	1	6-A	
3.5.4 Change header and footer size	1	6-A	
3.6 Create and apply cell styles			
3.6.1 Apply cell styles	1	4-E	4-5
3.6.2 Construct new cell styles	1	4-E	
4. Managing Worksheets and Workbooks			
4.1 Create and format worksheets			
4.1.1 Insert worksheets			
4.1.1.1 Single	1	5-A	
4.1.1.2 Multiple	1	5-A	
4.1.2 Delete worksheets			
4.1.2.1 Single	1	5-A	
4.1.2.2 Multiple	1	5-A	
4.1.3 Reposition worksheets	1	5-A	5-2
4.1.4 Copy worksheets	1	5-A	5-2
4.1.5 Move worksheets	1	5-A	
4.1.6 Rename worksheets	1	5-A	5-1
4.1.7 Group worksheets	1	5-A	
4.1.8 Apply color to worksheet tabs	1	5-A	5-1
4.1.9 Hide worksheet tabs	1	5-A	5-2
4.1.10 Unhide worksheet tabs	1	5-A	5-2
4.2 Manipulate window views			
4.2.1 Split window views	1	5-B	5-3

Objective Domain	Level	Topic	Activity
4.2.2 Arrange window views	1	5-B	5-3
4.2.3 Open a new window with contents from the current worksheet	1	5-B	5-3
4.3 Manipulate workbook views			
4.3.1 Use Normal workbook view	1	1-A	1-1
4.3.2 Use Page Layout workbook view	1	6-A	6-1
4.3.3 Use Page Break workbook view	1	6-A	6-1
4.3.4 Create custom views	2	6-B	
5. Applying Formulas and Functions			
5.1 Create formulas			
5.1.1 Use basic operators	1	2-A	2–1
5.1.2 Revise formulas	2	1-A	
5.2 Enforce precedence			
5.2.1 Order of evaluation	1	2-A	
5.2.2 Precedence using parentheses	1	2-A	
5.2.3 Precedence of operators for percent vs. exponentiation	2	1-C	
5.3 Apply cell references in formulas.			
5.3.1 Relative and absolute references	1	2-C	2-3
5.4 Apply conditional logic in a formula			
5.4.1 Create a formula with values that match conditions	2	1-D	
5.4.3 Use a series of conditional logic values in a formula	2	1-D	
5.5 Apply named ranges in formulas.			
5.5.1 Define ranges in formulas	2	1-A	1-1
5.5.2 Edit ranges in formulas	2	1-A	
5.5.3 Rename a named range	2	1-A	1-1
5.6 Apply cell ranges in formulas			
5.6.1 Enter a cell range definition in the formula bar	1	3-B	
5.6.2 Define a cell range	1	3-B	3-2
6. Presenting Data Visually			
6.1 Create charts based on worksheet data	2	3-A	3-1
6.2 Apply and manipulate illustrations			
6.2.1 Insert	2	5-A	5-1
6.2.2 Position	2	5-B	
6.2.3 Size	2	5-A, 5-B	5-1, 5-2
6.2.4 Rotate	2	5-B	
6.2.5 Modify Clip Art SmartArt	2	5-C	5-3
6.2.6 Modify Shape	2	5-B	5-2

Objective Domain	Level	Topic	Activity
6.2.7 Modify Screenshots	2	5-A	
6.3 Create and modify images by using the Image Editor			
6.3.1 Make corrections to an image			
6.3.1.1 Sharpen or soften an image	2	5-A	
6.3.1.2 Change brightness	2	5-A	
6.3.1.3 Change contrast	2	5-A	
6.3.2 Use picture color tools	2	5-A	
6.3.3 Change artistic effects on an image	2	5-A	
6.4 Apply Sparklines			
6.4.1 Use Line chart types	3	4-B	4-2
6.4.2 Use Column chart types	3	4-B	
6.4.3 Use Win/Loss chart types	3	4-B	
6.4.4 Create a Sparkline chart	3	4-B	
6.4.5 Customize a Sparkline	3	4-B	
6.4.6 Format a Sparkline	3	4-B	4-2
6.4.7 Show or hiding data markers	3	4-B	4-2
7. Sharing Worksheet Data with other users			
7.1 Share spreadsheets by using Backstage			
7.1.1 Send a worksheet via Email or Skydrive	2	2-B	2-5
7.1.2 Change the file type to a different version of Excel	1	1-D	1-4
7.1.3 Save as PDF or XPS	2	2-B	
7.2 Manage comments			
7.2.1 Insert	2	6-B	6-2
7.2.2 View	2	6-B	
7.2.3 Edit	2	6-B	6-2
7.2.4 Delete comments	2	6-B	
8. Analyzing and Organizing Data			
8.1 Filter data			
8.1.1 Define a filter	2	2-C	2-4
8.1.2 Apply a filter	2	2-C	2-4
8.1.3 Remove a filter	2	2-C	
8.1.4 Filter lists using AutoFilter	2,	2-C	2-4
8.2 Sort data			
8.2.1 Use sort options			
8.2.1.1 Values	2	2-C	2-4
8.2.1.2 Font color	2	2-C	
8.2.1.3 Cell color	2	2-C	
8.3 Apply conditional formatting			

Objective Domain	Level	Topic	Activity
8.3.1 Apply conditional formatting to cells	3	1-D	1-4
8.3.2 Use the Rule Manager to apply conditional formats	3	1-D	1-4
8.3.3 Use the IF function to apply conditional formatting	3	1-D	
8.3.4 Clear rules	3	1-D	
8.3.5 Use icon sets	3	1-D	
8.3.6 Use data bars	3	1-D	

Lesson Labs

Lesson labs are provided as an additional learning resource for this course. The labs may or may not be performed as part of the classroom activities. Your instructor will consider setup issues, classroom timing issues, and instructional needs to determine which labs are appropriate for you to perform, and at what point during the class. If you do not perform the labs in class, your instructor can tell you if you can perform them independently as self-study, and if there are any special setup requirements.

Lesson 1 Lab 1

Creating a Basic Worksheet Using Excel 2010

Activity Time: 10 minutes

Scenario:

You are the Human Resources manager of the Everything for Coffee company. Using an Excel spreadsheet, you want to analyze the employee information of your organization.

Name	Emp ID	Hire Date	Date of Birth	Branch Location	Hourly Wage
Miller	2605	05/03/2010	03/15/1978	New York	32
Doyle	2618	05/02/2010	05/17/1982	Boston	22
Johnson	2622	08/05/2010	07/02/1986	Seattle	22

1. Launch the Microsoft Excel 2010 application.

2. Create headers named *Name, Employee ID, Hire Date, Date of Birth, Branch Location,* and *Hourly Wage* in row 2 of columns A, B, C, D, E, and F, respectively.

3. Enter the labels, *Miller, Doyle,* and *Johnson* in the Name column, in cells A3, A4, and A5, respectively.

4. Enter the information for each employee in the corresponding cells in the worksheet as per the details provided in the scenario.

5. Perform a compatibility check on the worksheet.

6. Save the workbook as *My Employee Information.xlsx* and also save a copy in the XLS format.

Lesson 2 Lab 1
Executing Formulas and Functions

Activity Time: 15 minutes

Data Files:

C:\084576Data\Performing Calculations in an Excel Worksheet\Sales Summary.xlsx, enus_084576_02_1_datafiles.zip

Scenario:

You are the sales executive of the Everything for Coffee company. You have to track the company's sales values for the four quarters in an Excel worksheet. You also need to analyze the sales performance of your team and hand it over to your manager.

1. Use the AutoSum feature to calculate the total sales for the first quarter in cell E22.

2. Copy the formula to calculate the total sales to the cell range F22:H22.

3. Calculate the maximum sales for all four quarters in row 23.

4. Calculate the commission amount paid for each quarter at the rate specified in cell K2 in row 24.

5. Save the workbook as *My Sales Summary.xlsx* and close it.

Lesson 3 Lab 1

Reorganizing a Worksheet

Activity Time: 10 minutes

Data Files:

C:\084576Data\Modifying an Excel Worksheet\Everything for Coffee.xlsx, enus_084576_03_1_datafiles.zip

Scenario:

You are the sales executive of the Everything for Coffee company. You have tracked the company's projected sales values for the first half of the year on an Excel worksheet. You want to make the following modifications to the worksheet before sending it to your manager.

● Display the cost price value next to the relevant label.

● Create additional columns for February through June and fill in the sales values.

● Include two other items: Percolator and Chocolate.

● Change the specialty item to a more detailed name.

● Correct an incorrect subtitle in the spreadsheet.

● Spell check the entire spreadsheet and save a copy of the workbook with the changes made.

---

1.   Open the Everything for Coffee.xlsx file from the C:\084576Data\Modifying an Excel Worksheet folder.

---

2.   Move the cost price value in cell D13 to the respective row.

---

3.   Add columns after January for February through June and enter their sales values as *100, 85, 150, 175,* and *210,* respectively.

---

4.   Insert two rows below the existing row 10 to include two more items namely *Percolator* and *Chocolate.*

---

5.   Include the prices for Percolator and Chocolate as *162* and *32,* respectively, in the Price column.

---

6.   Edit cell A8 so that it reads *Specialty Coffee.*

---

7.   Replace the word "protected" with "projected."

---

8.   Spell check the worksheet and correct the misspelled words.

---

9. Save the file as *My Everything for Coffee.xlsx* and close it.

Lesson 4 Lab 1
Enhancing a Worksheet

Activity Time: 10 minutes

Data Files:

C:\084576Data\Modifying the Appearance of a Worksheet \Sales Summary.xlsx, enus_084576_04_1_datafiles.zip

Scenario:

You have recorded the sales revenue generated by the employees of the Everything for Coffee company. You want to distinguish the column headings and the Total row from the rest of the content in the worksheet. You also want to emphasize the title of the worksheet to enhance the presentation before it is presented.

- Column heading format:
  - Font face, size, and style: Arial, 12 pt, Bold.
  - Align them with the respective cells.
- Use the **Thick Box Border** to distinguish the column headings and Totals row from the other worksheet information.
- Format currency values using the **Accounting** format so that the decimal points and the dollar signs are aligned in one column.

---

1. Modify the font face, size, and style of the column headings according to the company specification.

2. Align all the column headings to match the position in the respective cells.

3. Add the specified border to the column headings and Totals row.

4. Apply the **Heading 1** cell style to the title of the worksheet.

5. Apply the **Accounting** number format to the cell range that contains financial values.

---

6. Save the workbook as *My Sales Summary.xlsx* and close it.

Lesson 5 Lab 1
Managing Excel Workbooks

Activity Time: 10 minutes

Data Files:

C:\084576Data\Managing an Excel Workbook\Company Info.xlsx, enus_084576_05_1_ datafiles.zip

Scenario:

You have consolidated your company's sales information into a single workbook. The workbook contains five worksheets, and you decide to apply formatting to the worksheet tabs so that you can identify them easily. You also want to delete the blank worksheets from the workbook and organize the remaining worksheets in a particular order. In addition, you want to create a workbook out of the payroll information provided in one of the worksheets. In the new workbook, you want to freeze the column headings of the Payroll Info worksheet so that you will always be able to see the headings, even when you scroll through the worksheet.

1. Open the Company Info.xlsx file from the C:\084576Data\Managing an Excel Workbook folder.

2. Delete Sheet3 and Sheet5.

3. Name the worksheets, starting from the left, as *Programmers, Payroll Info,* and *Schedule.*

4. Reposition the worksheet tabs in the order specified below.
   a. Payroll Info
   b. Programmers
   c. Schedule

5. Color the worksheet tabs.

6. Open a new window with a view of the current workbook.

7. In the new workbook, freeze the column headings on the Payroll Info worksheet.

8. Save the workbook as **My Company Info.xlsx** and close it.

Lesson 6 Lab 1
Printing a Workbook

Activity Time: 10 minutes

Data Files:

C:\084576Data\Printing Excel Workbooks\Sales Summary.xlsx, enus_084576_06_1_ datafiles.zip

Scenario:

You have prepared a sales report for the Everything For Coffee company and want to distribute a printout of the report to your sales team. You want the first three columns of the worksheet to be displayed on each page of the printout and the page number to be displayed in the footer. You need to format the worksheet split so that the data for each quarter appears on separate pages in print.

1. Change the page orientation to **Landscape.**

2. Set rows 1 and 2 and columns A to D as the print title.

3. Set cells A3:H27 as the print area.

4. Add the page number to the footer.

5. Add page breaks after the data for every quarter.

6. Save the workbook as **My Sales Summary.xlsx.**

7. Preview and print the worksheet.

Glossary

absolute reference
A cell reference in a formula that does not change when the formula from one cell is copied to another.

active cell
A cell that is selected in a worksheet.

application window
The outer window of Excel that provides tools and commands for you to work with the Excel window.

arguments
The data provided to functions to perform calculations.

Auto Fill feature
A feature that fills a range of cells with data based on the selected cells.

AutoSum feature
A feature that allows you to quickly insert functions for mathematical and statistical analysis.

Backstage view
An interface element that contains a series of tabs that group similar commands. It also contains options to save, share, print, and publish workbooks.

cell style
A collection of format options that you can apply to selected cells.

cells
The elements in a spreadsheet that store data.

Compatibility Checker feature
A feature that allows you to identify the compatibility of objects and data that are saved in an earlier version of Excel.

contextual tabs
The additional tabs that appear on the Ribbon when specific objects such as charts, tables, drawings, and text boxes are selected.

contiguous range
A range of continuous cells that are adjacent to each other.

Excel Help window
A window that provides a quick and easy way to find answers to Excel-related questions.

Excel
An application in the Microsoft Office suite that provides tools and features for working with spreadsheet data.

fill handle
The box at the bottom-right corner of the selected cell or cell range that allows you to use the Auto Fill feature.

fills
The options that enable you to highlight certain cells that contain important data.

font
A predefined typeface that can be used to format data.

footer

A text or graphic block that is printed at the bottom of each page.

format painter

A tool that allows you to copy only the formatting to apply to another cell or cell range.

Formula Bar

An interface component of Excel that displays the selected cell name, content, and formulas.

formula

A standard procedure that symbolically represents a calculation.

function name

An abbreviated name of a function.

function

A built-in formula in Excel that is used to perform calculations.

gallery

A repository for elements of the same category for accessing styles and appearance settings to apply to objects.

header

A text or graphic block that is printed at the top of each page.

Indent

A data repositioning command that is used to ensure better spacing and readability.

live preview

A dynamic feature that allows you to preview how formatting options will look on a worksheet before you actually apply the selected formatting.

Mini toolbar

A toolbar that is displayed when data in a cell is selected, and provides easy and quick access to frequently used formatting commands.

mixed reference

A cell reference that includes an absolute and a relative reference.

noncontiguous range

A range of cells that includes cells that are not adjacent to each other.

page breaks

The lines that break a worksheet into separate pages for printing.

page margin

A boundary line that shows the amount of space between the worksheet data and the edge of the paper.

page orientation

The page layout settings that switch the layout of the content either vertically or horizontally on a printed page.

print area

The desired area in a worksheet that is selected for printing.

Quick Access toolbar

A customizable toolbar that provides easy access to frequently used commands in the application.

relative reference

A cell reference in a formula that changes when a formula from one cell is copied to another.

Ribbon

An interface component that enables you to perform various tasks in the Excel application without the need to navigate extensively.

spreadsheet

A paper or an electronic document that is used to store and manipulate different types of data in a tabular format.

status bar

An interface component that is located at the bottom of the application window that allows you to view and customize the layout of a worksheet.

template

A predesigned layout that is used in the creation of new documents.

typeface

The style or design of a set of characters.

workbook window

The inner window of Excel that contains the spreadsheet and the commands to work with data.

workbook

An Excel file that contains Excel worksheets.

worksheet

A worksheet is an electronic spreadsheet that contains rows and columns and stores various types of data in the Excel application.

Index